The Transc

Volume Three

The Transformed World and The Ego's World: "The Thunder of the Meaningless"

Kenneth Wapnick, Ph.D.

Foundation for A Course in Miracles®

Foundation for A Course in Miracles®
375 N Stephanie St, Suite 2311
Henderson, NV 89014
www.facim.org

Printed in the United States of America

First printing, 2022

ISBN 978-1-59142-951-7

The Transformed World

Introduction

The topic today is "The Transformed World." I do not think this term appears in the Course, but the concept certainly does, and the word "transformed" appears a great deal. As with many terms based on the Course, there are different levels of meaning. The ultimate meaning of the transformed world would be the real world, which one could say would be the actual goal of the Course. Once we are in the real world, then Heaven is just one step away.

The real world has nothing to do with the physical universe, of course. The real world is that state of mind in which total forgiveness has occurred and the Atonement has been accepted. We truly know, not just cognitively or intellectually, that the entire world is a dream; our physical existence in this world is a dream, and our reality is outside of the dream. When we know that once and for all and never waver, that is the real world. We can say the transformed world would be equivalent to that. There is a beautiful section called "The Forgiven World," which really is about the real world, in which the Holy Spirit is referred to as "the great Transformer of perception" (T-17.II.5:2). When that transformation is complete, that is the real world.

But the term also would be relevant for the process; the process wherein we go continually from our wrong minds to our right minds. And then we become afraid, we become wrong-minded again and embrace the ego as our teacher. Then we recognize that is a mistake, and we go back to Jesus or the Holy Spirit. It is that process back and forth that is a gradual transforming of our perception.

There is a workbook lesson that says: "Let miracles replace all grievances" (W-pI.78). As we let go of our grievances one by one, that is a transformation of the relationship. Someone that heretofore we had hated or that we had made our special love object, all of a sudden we recognize is our true brother in Christ. The relationship then becomes transformed.

The ultimate goal of the Course, which actually is stated at the beginning of the workbook, is that we generalize these instants, these holy instants, when a miracle replaces a grievance, when we choose forgiveness instead of judgment. And we generalize it, not just to one person but to all persons; not to one person some of the time, but to all people all of the time. It is that process of generalization that goes into the gradual transformation of our perception or the transformation of our world. And again, when that is fully complete and forgiveness is fully consummated, that is the real world. That is the end of the journey. So today, as in the Course, we will go back and forth between both of these ideas.

A Shift in Perspective

What we are really talking about is a shift in perspective, a shift in how we look. When we talk about the world being transformed, once again, we are not talking about the physical world changing. We are not talking about the relationships in our lives necessarily changing in form. We are not talking about our lives getting better—getting better financially, getting better health wise. We are only talking about the mind because, as you know, the mind is all that there is. Since *ideas leave not their source* (T-26.VII.4:7;13:2), the thought of separation and the thought system of sin, guilt, and fear, attack, judgment, and death, and punishment that ensues from sin, guilt and fear—all of this can be put together as one single thought of the ego that has never left its source; meaning that projection does not work, which means there is no world out here (W-pI.132.6:2).

It would make no sense for a world to change when there was never a world to begin with. This is extremely important as a student of the Course, so that you do not confuse the Course with other spiritual teachings or other spiritual paths that do place a premium on things outside changing. The Course is not against things outside changing. It is saying that outside changes are irrelevant. There is that section in the manual, "Are Changes Required In The Life Situation Of God's Teachers?" (M-9), where Jesus makes the point that it is the internal change that is important, that change is necessary.

Again, if things change for the better externally, all well and good, but that has nothing to do with the peace of God. That has nothing to do with your Atonement path. And it has nothing to do with your awakening from the dream and returning home. All of that can only occur when your mind changes, which basically means we shift from the ego as our teacher to Jesus or the Holy Spirit as our Teacher. That is the transformation.

There are several passages in the Course where we are told that the Holy Spirit does not take our special relationships away from us (T-17.IV.2:3); He transforms them. In other words, He does not deal with the form of the relationship. By transforming it, what Jesus is really talking about is He changes our attitude about them. Relationships may or may not change. In fact, over time of course, they are going to change in form. But what needs to change is our attitude towards the relationship; more specifically, our attitude towards this person with whom we are in a relationship, regardless of the form of the relationship.

That is why there is absolutely nothing in *A Course in Miracles* about behavior. There is nothing in *A Course in Miracles* about changing anything externally. It is all about changing one's mind. The underlying metaphysics of the Course is that there is no world out here—this is a nondualistic system—there is God and there is nothing else. Within the dream that we think we exist in, the reflection of that principle is our right-minded thought system of forgiveness, which the

Course tells us is an "earthly form of love" (W-pI.186.14.2), or a reflection of love: love not being possible in this world. But forgiveness is the means of remembering that love. And that memory is in our right minds. It is in everyone's right mind.

It is in learning how to gain access to that love, learning how to gain access to that memory and begin to identify with it that is what the miracle is about. That is what forgiveness is about, indeed, what the teachings of *A Course in Miracles* are all about and are geared to having us make that shift. Our focus is never on behavior or the world. It is always on the thought that gave rise to the world. It is all about how we look at things.

There is that very important line in the teacher's manual. It is the section on magic thoughts where Jesus says, remember, you never get angry at a fact. You get angry at an interpretation of a fact (M-17.8:6). What we call facts, are what go on in the world—people's behaviors. Interpretation has to do with whether we look at what goes on in the world through our wrong mind, the thought system of judgment of the ego; or we look at it through the eyes of our right mind, which would be through the eyes of the Holy Spirit—forgiveness. That is interpretation.

We never get angry at a fact. It is the interpretation we give the fact that makes us angry, which means we are never angry with what goes on outside. Because again, in the end, nothing goes on outside. We are angry because we have chosen the teacher of anger. If we are truly at peace, it is because we have chosen the Teacher of peace. Again, it is never what goes on outside. I say repeatedly, probably in every class, that that is where the confusion enters into in terms of students of this course and teachers of this course. They do not fully recognize the distinction between mind and body.

This is not a course about the body at all. It talks to us as if we were bodies because we believe we are bodies. So it would talk about transforming the world or saving the world or healing the world or being the light of the world, and we automatically think of behavior. We think of persons. We think of special functions, special missions, special people, special abilities, and they are all external.

Again, to be sure, the language of the Course seems to reflect that. And you will become confused only when you forget other passages where, in effect, Jesus says I must speak to you in "the condition in which" you think you are, which is a body (T-25.I.7:4). He tells us in the introduction to the clarification of terms: "This course remains within the ego framework" (C-in.3:1). Meaning, it consists of words, it consists of concepts, and it is pitched to what we believe to be our experience in the world as bodies. We are not bodies. Why? Because *ideas leave not their source* (T-26.VII.4:7,13:2; W-pI.132.5:3,10:3).

This is why I spend part of almost every workshop talking about this, because it is so easy to get confused. It is so easy to lapse back into believing this course is about me as a person, as a body forgiving this other person and body.

Kindness

We speak a great deal about kindness. I emphasize that a great deal in everything I teach. It seems to be, I should be kind to other people. Sure, we should be kind to other people. But we cannot be truly kind to other people if we do not first accept the Teacher of kindness in our minds. Otherwise, then, we could term this kindness-to-destroy, taking that from the term forgiveness-to-destroy in *The Song of Prayer* pamphlet.

Kindness-to-destroy is when it appears to be kindness, but it really reinforces duality. It really reinforces specialness. I am a person, and I am being kind to you, you poor, unfortunate wretch. And that is the principle, whether you articulate it or not, whether you are conscious of it or not, that underlies when you believe you are being kind to another person. There is no other person.

When you accept the Teacher of kindness as the only one you listen to, meaning the Holy Spirit or Jesus, the kindness inherent in that Presence in our right minds, the kindness inherent in that loving Thought that sees everyone as the same, will automatically extend through you with your doing nothing. It will just extend through you. And then that extension through you will guide your behavior, whether it is thinking, whether it is speaking or acting. It will guide your behavior to be kind. It is not something you have to do. It is something that is done through you.

In effect, what we have to do as students of *A Course in Miracles* is clear the decks of our mind. Clear it of all the impure thoughts, all the angry thoughts, judgmental thoughts, specialness thoughts; all the thoughts that would articulate somehow or specify that there is something to be done here and someone to do it. That is where you get trapped.

When you are right-minded, your body may be very busy, but you will have no identification with what your body does, and certainly no identification with how other bodies seem to relate to or respond to what your body does—what you say, what you write, how you act. Because you would truly begin to understand that you are not the body. You are not the person through whom this kindness and this love are coming through.

What this really is all about is that we transform our minds, which really means we simply change teachers. Over and over again, we are told how very simple this course is and how very simple its practice is. It comes down very simply to which teacher do I choose? And the decision for my inner teacher is predicated on what my goal is. Is my goal to remain in the dream; to remain a special person, an individual with special gifts, special talents, special abilities, special functions, special missions? Or is my goal to awaken from the dream—to awaken from the dream of specificity and embrace the abstract Thought that created me? Since *ideas leave not their source*, since God's Son has never left his Father, we are that abstract Reality. We are that abstract Thought, spelled with a capital "T."

Anything that reinforces my specific identity, my specific existence, my specific job, my specific mission if I think I have one; my specific work, my specific relationships, will end up reinforcing the very thing you are saying you want to awaken from. That is one way of understanding what transformation is. It is transforming how you see the world, not transforming the world.

"Projection makes perception" (T-13.V.3:5; T-21.in.1:1). That is such a key principle in the Course. In fact, it is one of the very few phrases that is repeated. *Projection makes perception.* What that means is, I look within, I choose a thought system with which I will identify, and I project that out. If it is wrong-minded, we use the word *projection.* If it is right-minded, we use the word *extension.* But in the original dictation to Helen, Jesus talked about extension as the appropriate use of projection, and what is now called projection the inappropriate use of projection. That was obviously a little clunky, and it became much more simply: The ego projects and the Holy Spirit extends. But the dynamic is exactly the same. *Projection makes perception.*

One can just as easily say *extension makes perception.* If I look within and I see guilt, then that is what I will project out and that is what I will see all around me. If I look within and I see guiltlessness, the innocence of God's Son who has never separated, then everything I see outside will be innocent and guiltless, despite what people may do. This is not saying that in the world, in our dream, people do not do cruel and malicious things. They do. But the original ego thought is cruel and malicious, not to mention horribly selfish and self-centered. We do not care about God. We do not care about His Son. We only care about our identity.

The Simplicity of Salvation

Let me read one very, very nice passage that makes this very clear. It is near the end of the text, page 646, paragraph 7.

While the term *projection* does not appear in this passage and certainly, therefore, the statement *projection makes perception*, this is the content behind these words. And again, it is very, very clear.

(T-31.I.7:1-8) The lessons to be learned are only two. Each has its outcome in a different world. And each world follows surely from its source. The certain outcome of the lesson that God's Son is guilty is the world you see. It is a world of terror and despair. Nor is there hope of happiness in it. There is no plan for safety you can make that ever will succeed. There is no joy that you can seek for here and hope to find.

That is *projection makes perception.* If I make guilt real, meaning I believe the separation from God happened, if I believe that, it is impossible not to feel I have sinned; it is impossible not to feel guilty, overwhelmed with the guilt of what I have done. I have not only destroyed God, I have destroyed Heaven. Because how could a state of separation exist in perfect Oneness? And if I believe I exist, there can be no perfect Oneness. That is what the Course refers to as the crucifixion of God's Son. It has nothing to do with the Christian myth. The crucifixion of God's Son is what occurred in the separation. He ceased to exist. He ceased to be.

Whenever we believe we exist as separate beings, separate entities, we are saying, "I am a sinner." I am overwhelmed with guilt, and my guilt demands I be punished. I am terrified of the inevitability of the punishment that must come from God because He is the One I sinned against. The only way I can escape from that is to project it out, magically believing what I project out I get rid of. When I project the contents of my mind outward, it gives rise to a world. That is what we all did at the beginning as one Son. That is how the cosmos was made. And that is how we continually make up our world, moment by moment.

Every time I choose the ego as my teacher, which means I choose to believe in the reality of separation, I am buying the whole kit and caboodle of the ego thought system. It is a perfectly consistent and internally coherent thought system. If you accept one part of that thought system as real, you must accept all of it as real, because it is internally consistent and coherent within itself. It is insane. But there is a logic to a paranoid thought system, as an example. There is a logic to insane thinking.

When you understand the logic, everything makes perfect sense. It may be insane, but you can at least understand what the fantasies are about, what the delusional thinking is about, what the hallucinations are about that follow from it, because you understand the logic. Well, the ego is a perfectly logical system. Once you accept its basic premise that the separation happened, every step follows logically from there. And if you believe one part of it, you believe all of it.

Just as on the other side, Jesus says, you either believe all of this course or none of it (T-22.II.7:4). That is what he says. You either believe all of it or none of it. Now that does not mean as a student, you cannot pick and choose what you are comfortable with. But just be aware that is what you are doing. This part of the Course makes me uncomfortable. This part of the Course I do not agree with; it does not agree with my theology. But this part of the Course is really helpful to me.

There is nothing wrong in doing that, but it is no longer *A Course in Miracles*. It is *A Course in Miracles* according to "__" and put your name in it. That is not a sin. It is just another spirituality. But what is really important to understand is that you not judge yourself or judge others who do that.

A lot of people say I do not like the metaphysics of the Course, but I do love its teaching of forgiveness. I do love what it says about giving up judgment. I do love where it says God is the only reality. I do love where it says that I should not do anything without asking the Holy Spirit or Jesus first. So that is the part of the Course that you work with, and you discount all the other statements about the body not being real, we are not even here, this never happened—time never happened, etc. And again, there is nothing wrong in doing that, but it is not *A Course in Miracles*. It is something else.

There is nothing wrong with eclectic spirituality if that works for you, but do not call it *A Course in Miracles*, because then you are doing yourself a disservice and you are doing the Course a disservice. Please do not feel guilty if you pick and choose and do not be judgmental of other people who pick and choose. Respect their spirituality and respect their thought system. And respect your own and stay with your own.

Many of you know the line I have quoted many, many times that Jesus once said to Helen when she was getting very upset about somebody teaching the Course incorrectly. He said to her, "Do not take another's path as your own, but neither should you judge it." Stay true to what you believe the Course is saying and stay true to your spiritual path, but do not judge other people who are doing something else. If they are teaching *A Course in Miracles* according to a standard you judge as being incorrect, that is their spirituality. What right do you have to tell them not to do that? If it works for them, if it makes them kinder and more loving, what could be wrong with that? But it is not *A Course in Miracles*.

When you choose guilt as your teacher, you will inevitably look on a guilty world. And you know you are doing that if you believe you are a person. If you believe you are a person studying a book called *A Course in Miracles*, then you are saying the ego is right. Separation is real. I am a separate person studying a separate thing called *A Course in Miracles*. I have my own separate teacher named the Holy Spirit or Jesus. Separation, separation, separation: body, body, body. Now that does not mean that that will not help you, but you will not get home, at least not according to the Course's way.

Again, there are thousands of other ways, including thousands of other ways of looking at *A Course in Miracles*. But it is all of one piece. Just as you cannot separate out parts of the Course and still say it is *A Course in Miracles*, you cannot separate out parts of your ego and say, "Well, this is not the ego." Anything that is specific, anything that is separating is of the ego, unless you are using it as a classroom in which you learn that you are not separated, which, of course, is what the whole Course is about in terms of practice. We use our ego thought system, we use our ego experiences, we use our special relationships as the classrooms in which we learn that there is no ego.

There is one statement that says that the purpose of time is to teach us there is no time. Now that is not how and why time was made. Time was made to perpetuate the illusion of linearity, which is the illusion of separation. But once we made time that way, the Holy Spirit uses time to collapse it, and uses time to lead us to the holy instant. What the ego made to hurt, the Holy Spirit uses to help. So that is a right-minded use of the illusion. It still remains an illusion, but it now serves a different purpose.

But if we look within our minds and we make guilt real, then we will feel that we are inadequate, we will feel that we are inferior, and we will put those abstract feelings onto specific things. I am guilty because I was a bad boy or girl. I am guilty because I cheated on my income tax. I am guilty because I cheated on this person. I am guilty because I am not a good *Course in Miracles*' student. I am guilty because I did not do my workbook lesson. We affix that guilt to specific things. Nonetheless, what is underneath those specific forms is the overriding thought, I sinned against God. And I know I did because I think there is an "I."

Once we do that, it is inevitable that we would look out on a world of terror and despair without any hope of happiness. A world in which we are not safe and that nothing will ever work. This then becomes "a dry and dusty place where starved and thirsty creatures come to die" (W-pII.13.5:1). The only way they can preserve their little life a little bit longer is to cannibalize other people. We cannibalize other living things to eat physically, and we cannibalize other people to meet our own special needs. That is what preserves our existence just a little bit longer in this dry and dusty world in which starved and thirsty creatures come to die.

When we look out on a world and it strikes terror in our hearts, when we hear things in the news that make us frightened or make us angry, or things happen in our personal world that make us frightened, that make us despairing, that make us feel depressed, that make us feel that loss is the reality; what this course is asking us to do is to take those experiences and those perceptions and those judgments and bring them back to their source. Sentence 3 again:

(T-31.I.7:3)...each world follows surely from its source.

That is what is in back of Lesson 5, even though the description in Lesson 5 does not seem that profound. "I am never upset for the reason I think." I am never upset for the reason I think is because there is nothing out there that can upset me. There is nothing out there. That cannot be said too often. Even if you cannot wrap yourself around that, you may intellectually accept it, but certainly it is not part of your experience, at least know that that is there. That is what this course is based on. Otherwise, there is no forgiveness that is possible except the ego's forgiveness-to-destroy.

Forgiveness is not possible if you think there is something and someone out there to forgive. That is the ultimate meaning of the Course's description of forgiveness. You forgive your brother for what he has not done. Within the world of our everyday experience, what he has not done is that he has not taken the peace of God away from me. But ultimately, he has not done it because there is nobody out there to do anything. He does not have a body to do something with. I am not a body that what he does can affect. What has to be changed, what has to be transformed is the teacher I have chosen. Let us continue on:

(T-31.I.7:9) Yet this is not the only outcome which your learning can produce.

That is because we not only have a wrong mind; we have a right mind. One of the real, real goals of the workbook (it is not actually stated this way, but it is implicit all the way through—it is like a thread that winds its way through the whole workbook), is that we really come away from it after the one-year training program knowing that we have a mind, and that the mind is split. It is split between two mutually exclusive thought systems—the ego's or the Holy Spirit's. And we can choose which one we will identify with. That is what the workbook will help you do.

Why is there no past, as the early lessons say and emphasize? There is no past because there is no body and there is no world. There is a mind that makes up the past. Since there is no time, my mind is making up my past right now. It is making up my seeming present right now, let alone what I think will happen in the future. Everything is the mind, and the mind is outside of time and space.

What is really helpful—and this passage is based on that, as indeed all of the Course is—is that there is a split mind that we have within the dream. In Heaven, there is only one Mind. But in the dream, there is a split mind: an ego and a Holy Spirit. That is where the transformation occurs in the decision-making part of the mind that chooses between these two thoughts. And from these two thoughts arise two different worlds. We have seen the first world—a world of terror and despair, etc.

(T-31.I.7:10) However much you may have overlearned your chosen task [that is a psychological and educational term—*overlearning*—that means you learn something over and over and over again. We have overlearned how to drive our car, how to tie our shoelaces, how to shave, how to wash one's hair. These are things we do over and over again. We do not even think about it, which makes it very difficult to break the habit, because it is something that we have overlearned. However much you may have overlearned your chosen task], **the lesson that reflects the Love of God is stronger still.**

The attraction of love is stronger than the attraction of fear or guilt. The attraction of returning to eternal life is stronger than the attraction of death. Otherwise, there would be no hope. Even when we consistently choose the ego, the attraction of love is still stronger. That is where the hope lies. The pull to the light is stronger than the pull to darkness, even when we seem to live in darkness. That is what this is saying, and that is what this whole course is based on.

That is what Jesus is consistently appealing to. He is not appealing to you as a person that you forgive this other person or that you ask his help regarding what you should do in a particular situation. He is appealing to your decision-making mind to let the natural attraction of love for love (T-12.VIII) be there. Do not cover it over because it is so strong that the effort to conceal it must be equally as strong. That is why you get sick. That is why you get upset. That is why you get depressed. That is why you get angry. That is why you get fearful.

Because: you are expending tremendous effort in pushing love away, even though love is there, because you are denying reality. It takes tremendous effort to deny reality. It does not seem like it because we are so used to it. It takes tremendous effort to believe we are here. If the attraction of love for love in our right mind is so strong and it pulls the decision maker right into it, to fight against that to preserve our individual identity requires tremendous effort, *tremendous effort.*

At the beginning of the section called "The Simplicity of Salvation" (T-31.I), Jesus is addressing Helen and Bill. But he is obviously addressing all of us and saying, "Do not tell me you cannot learn this course. Do not tell me it is so difficult. Look what you have taught yourself." How could you possibly doubt the power of your learning skill? Look what you have taught yourself.

You have taught yourself to deny reality; first in thought, then you construct this universe that seems massive. Then you believe in it. And then you construct a whole series of relationships and experiences and bodies to prove that the impossible has happened, and that reality is not true. That requires tremendous effort, because we are denying what is true. We are denying the love that created us and the love that we are—a love embracing everyone and everything without exception. It requires tremendous effort to continually judge.

There is a line (T-13.III.3:1) where Jesus says: is it not easier to say "I hate" rather than "I love?" Of course it is—much easier. Because that is who we think we are, children of hate, because we think we are children of guilt. We deny this power and we deny this love. Of course, this is not a power as the world knows it. The purpose of this course is to restore to our awareness this tremendous attraction of love for love.

At the end of "The Obstacles to Peace," Jesus says this love calls to us from beyond the veil (T-19.IV.D.19,21). And we are continually pushing it away. There is a passage in the text that says truth calls, and you always answer with a substitute (T-17.IV.3:2). How much easier it is just to answer truth's call, love's call and say, "Yes, here I am." We do not do that. We answer with a substitute. That requires tremendous energy, effort and constant vigilance. Because the love will always break through if we are not careful. That is why we made a world and a body to distract us so completely that that attraction in our mind seems forever buried. But it is there.

And when we learn that there is another Presence in our mind that we are really attracted to:

(T-31.I.7:11)...you will learn God's Son is innocent, and [then you will] **see another world.**

That is the transformed world. And what is this world like?

(T-31.I.8:1) The outcome of the lesson that God's Son is guiltless is a world in which there is no fear, and everything is lit with hope and sparkles with a gentle friendliness.

Now, if your world does not feel like this, it is not the world's fault. If your world does not reflect what I just read (and I will continue in a moment), it is because your mind has chosen a different source for it to perceive a different world. *I am never upset for the reason I think* (W-pI.5). This world is a world of hate because it was conceived in hate. The Course says "The world was made as an attack on God"—that is pretty hateful (W-pII.3.2:1).

If it is an attack on God, it is an attack on His Son. As bodies, we walk this world continually attacking God's Son, sometimes protesting that we love him—special love—more often than not, hating. But one could walk in this world of hate and still feel that "everything is lit with hope." There is no fear, and everything "sparkles with a gentle friendliness." Why? Because you have made Jesus your *only* friend. And when you make him your only friend, everyone becomes your friend because his love embraces everyone.

The ego's love only embraces one person: itself. And it seems to love those who reinforce the ego self. That is what the Course calls specialness. You meet my need and I love you. You do not meet my need, and I hate you. And I will crucify you. I will badmouth you. I will judge you. I will criticize you. I will hurt you. I will kill you. But when you meet my need, I love you.

(T-31.I.8:2-5) Nothing but calls to you in soft appeal to be your friend, and let it join with you. And never does a call remain unheard, misunderstood, nor left unanswered in the selfsame tongue in which the call was made. And you will understand it was this call that everyone and everything within the world has always made, but you had not perceived it as it was. And now you see you were mistaken.

Everyone has a right mind. That is what this is saying. Everyone has a right mind that calls to us. Everyone has a right mind that calls to us and says, "Please show me I am wrong. Please show me that I was wrong in choosing the ego. Please show me that the world is not a place of hopelessness and despair, of darkness, depression and death. Please show me that attack is not salvation. Please show me that guilt is not the comforting blanket I thought it was. Please show me I was wrong." That is what you will hear. That is what this is saying.

(T-31.I.8:2) Nothing [in this world] **but calls to you in soft appeal to be your friend…**

Be my friend, not my enemy. Do not join me on the dance floor of death. Do not trade tit for tat with me. Do not judge me just because I attack you. Please do not punish me because I have said something unkind to you or to your loved ones. Please do not invade my country. Please, please show me I was wrong in coveting specialness instead of love. That is what you will hear. How could this world not be beautiful if that is all you hear?

"Nothing but calls to you in soft appeal to be your friend, and let it join with you": because you and I are the same. I keep trying to prove that you are different. I keep judging you and attacking you and abusing you and victimizing you. I want you to be sane because I cannot be sane. And I want you, by your defenselessness and your forgiveness and your love, to show me that I am wrong. Witness to me there is another thought system. That is what everybody's attack on you is saying, if you listen.

And you will listen if you first listen to Jesus' voice in your mind. If you first listen to the Holy Spirit's thought system of Atonement that says the separation never happened, which means you and I are not separate. Our bodies seem separate because bodies were made to be separate. But perception lies: *Nothing so blinding as perception of form* (T-22.III.6:7). Form lies. People's words lie. Their thoughts lie. Their behaviors lie. Everybody lies. Because they all come from an inner perception, an inner thought of separation. And what you make real in your mind you must—*must*—perceive outside, because there is nothing outside.

What seems to be outside has come from inside. *Ideas leave not their source* (T-26.VII.4:7,13:2). If I want to know how I am doing, if I want to know which teacher I am choosing, I just have to pay attention to my perceptions. They will tell me. If I do not perceive the universal sameness of God's Son, if I do not see everyone having the same split mind that I do (wrong mind, right mind, decision maker); if I do not see that, I must be coming from my ego.

What has to be transformed is not *you*, not my situation, not my education, not my work, not my relationships, not my body. What has to be transformed is my thinking. Now this makes no sense unless you realize that this course is addressed to you as a mind, not a body. Nothing I have said, nothing that is in this book will make sense, even though you may think it makes sense, if you do not recognize this is all and only about the mind and not the body. That is what it is going to say in a minute. Let me read sentences 4 and 5 and then go on.

(T-31.I.8:4-7) And you will understand it was this call [to please show me that I am wrong] **that everyone and everything within the world has always made, but you had not perceived it as it was. And now you see you were mistaken.** [Why? How did that happen?] **You had been deceived by forms the call was hidden in. And so you did not hear it, and had lost a friend who always wanted to be part of you.**

You had been deceived by forms the call was hidden in. You did not hear the call. You did not hear the right-minded plaintive call that says, "Please show me I am wrong. I am so insane I cannot help attacking you. I cannot help coveting more and more specialness from you. I cannot help being dependent on you to take care of me. I cannot help making judgments about you and everyone else. I cannot help it. Please show me there is another way because I am so dense in my thinking, I am so terrified, I cannot see it."

That is the call. That is what is in back of the earlier statement in the text that the Holy Spirit only sees expressions of love or calls for love. But if you are stuck with the form, because you think you are a form, i.e., a body, you will not hear the call.

(T-31.I.8:6) You had been deceived by forms the call was hidden in.

To play a little with words, you want to transform the form, meaning you want to transform your perception of the form, not the form itself. I do not want to change you; my ego wants to change you. I want to change how I perceive you.

Over many, many years of working with couples and families, people would often come to me when their relationship seemed to be in bad shape and divorce was imminent. I would say, "Before you make a decision about whether to leave or stay, I don't care what you do, as long as you do it peacefully." Without using these words the content of what I would say is, transform your perception before you do anything on the level of form. Relationships are not images graven in stone. God did not ordain marriages. Nothing is forever. But you want to make peace forever. You want to make love forever.

Before you could know what is the right-minded way to end or transform or renew a relationship, renew and transform your mind. Then you will know that I should stay with this person or leave this person, and there will be no guilt. There will be no projection, no anxiety, no anger, no judgment, and no sense of loss. Relationships in form are not eternal.

The love in your mind is eternal. But when you are deceived by the form, you will not hear the call. And indeed, you will believe that distinctions and differentiations are real and justified. They become legitimate because we think we are bodies, and bodies have to judge among forms. We all have to judge where we would be today. We all have to judge what we would eat, where we would eat, what we would wear, where we would sit, whom we sit next to, whom we do not want to sit next to. We all make judgments. You cannot exist in this world unless you make judgments.

But they do not have to be attacking. They do not have to be exclusive. They do not have to be investments. But if any of the things I have mentioned become an issue (the clothes you wear, the food you eat, etc., etc.), then you want to ask the great Transformer of perception to help you transform your perception. Well, if *projection makes perception*, I cannot transform my perception unless I transform what it is I am projecting, which is my mind's decision for the ego or the Holy Spirit.

We all have to do things in this world. We all have to have relationships. We have families. We have to do things for our families. We have to do things with our jobs or businesses. We have to do things with our bodies. But you can do it either from a wrong-minded or a right-minded perspective. And you know you have chosen your wrong mind if you are anxious, if you are tense, if you are nervous, if you are upset. It is very, very simple.

(T-31.I.8:8) The soft eternal calling of each part of God's creation to the whole is heard throughout the world this second lesson brings.

"Each part." Above, it said "everyone and everything." That is the key. That is how you know which teacher you have chosen. It is very, very simple. If you are invested in something you do or something someone else does that differentiates them from other people, know that is your ego. If you are invested in something specific that you do or ought to do or other people do, and it becomes important to you and you believe it is significant, know that is your ego.

Some people will think it is more significant in the world to teach *A Course in Miracles* than to fix a broken pipe as a plumber. That is how you know there is something wrong with your thinking, because you are not seeing everyone and everything as the same. If you see everyone and everything as the same, you will not say there is a hierarchy of illusions, which is the first law of chaos (T-23.II.2:3). You will not say there is a hierarchy of professions or functions or anything in this world, because everything would be the same. You either choose the ego as your teacher or the Holy Spirit as your Teacher. End of story. And you will realize that that is what everyone is doing in this world. That is the only thing you focus on.

If someone is obviously coming from their ego because they are being judgmental and exclusive and separating, not to mention attacking, then you hear that call from their right mind—the soft eternal calling of each part of God's creation. You will hear that call that says, "Please show me I am wrong." And then you will demonstrate the reality of the thought system that is the source of your defenselessness, your genuine kindness, your love that is not changed by other people's attacks or other people's "loving" things that they do. That is what you transform. That is how the world is transformed. It all depends on how you look at it. Everything depends how you look at it. You can see the world as being a harmful place; you can see it as being a kind and helpful place.

Let me tell you a very, very quick example. My wife, Gloria, is home sick with bronchitis. The other day I bent down to kiss her and she said, "Don't kiss me, you'll get my germs." And I said, "No, if I kiss you, you'll get my health." It is the exact same activity. It depends on where you start. It depends what your source is. The world does not change out there. How could what is not out there change? Just think about it. That is why, I have been saying for thirty-five years, when you study this course, do not leave the metaphysics too far behind. Because if you do, you will get so confused over what this course is saying. If there is no world out there, why do you care what happens out there? Which, is not an invitation to be insensitive, callous and indifferent to people's suffering, just the opposite.

You cannot be callous, insensitive and indifferent to people's sufferings if you are coming from a loving place in your mind. Then that love within you that you are now identified with, which forgiveness opens up, embraces everyone. And you will be kind and loving and thoughtful in the very form that the person who is suffering needs you to be kind, loving and thoughtful. It does not mean, again, that you turn your back on people's suffering with that kind of metaphysical sweep of the hand that says, "Oh, nothing is happening anyway." That is denial and that is hateful. That is not loving. Love will always assume the form that is the most helpful, even if it may not look like that.

"See It as Soup"

It all depends on how you look at things. Let me tell you another story. It is another Gloria story. It is a cute story, and actually I have been meaning to tell this story for about eighteen, nineteen years when it first happened. I do not know why I keep forgetting. I said to myself this morning, I am not going to forget it today, because it fits. Gloria is a wonderful cook. There are very few Italians who are not wonderful cooks. And those of you who used to go to Roscoe know when she used to cook in the kitchen. One of the things that she makes very, very well is escarole. And she takes escarole and she sautés garlic and the escarole in olive oil, and it is wonderful. You never get it like that in a restaurant.

So she made that one day and there were leftovers. The next day, she heated it up. And one of the things that she does not do well as a cook that I always remind her is that she sometimes puts too much water when she heats things up. So she serves the escarole and it is all water. And I said, "You ruined it. This was so wonderful yesterday." And she said to me, "See it as escarole soup." [Laughter] That is exactly what she said.

So I took it from my flat plate and I put it in a bowl, and instead of eating it with a fork I ate it with a soup spoon, and it was delicious. It did not change. That is the truth. It did not change. I changed. My mind set was no longer a vegetable that was kind of sloshing around in my plate. It was now soup. And it was wonderful as a soup, with the garlic and the oil. It was heavenly.

The world does not change; our attitude changes. That is a cute little story which would seem to have no real importance. But when you generalize it, and when you see someone attacking you and you get angry, you are seeing them as a sloshy piece of escarole. [Laughter] See it as soup. See the person as soup, and you will love it. And that will help you not take your anger and your judgment so seriously. Think escarole, and you will not take your anger seriously, and you will not take your perceptions of evil and sin seriously. Think of it as just escarole soup, sloshing around in your plate. That is what evil is. That is what sin is. It is silly.

Every student of the Course knows the line: "Into eternity, where all is one, there crept a tiny, mad idea, at which the Son of God remembered not to laugh" (T-27.VIII.6:2). The tiny, mad idea is silly. It is not evil. It is not sinful. We chose the wrong teacher and that was *the* problem. The tiny, mad idea could not be the problem. It never happened. How could what never happened, how could an illusion be a problem?

But when we chose the ego, which is the part of us that likes being separated, the tiny, mad idea now became not only real; not only something that was possible, it became gargantuan. It had the power to destroy Heaven. That is when the idea of sin comes in. This is not a silly thought that meant nothing and is nothing. It now became a gargantuan thing, grandiose, magnificent.

We made our own self. We made our own god. We made our own world. We made our own love. We took it seriously, which meant we took our sin against God seriously. Guilt is what does that. Guilt says you not only have committed a heinous sin; you are a heinous person. It is not only that you have sinned; you are sin.

And like Lady Macbeth, you will never wash the stain of sin from your hands. *Never.* It is imprinted indelibly on your mind. And because of what you have done, you will be punished, just like the Bible says. Because of what you have done, God says to Adam and Eve, this is what will happen. And this tremendously cruel punishment ensues: suffering, death and total and eternal banishment from Heaven, from the Garden of Eden. That is what we all believe.

And if that were not insane enough, the ego's strategy is even more insane. We can get rid of this by projecting it out. The sin now is all around us. And it is heavy. It is fraught with guilt. It burdens us. Our shoulders sag; all because we remembered not to laugh at the tiny, mad idea. We thought we destroyed God and crucified His Son. And all that happened was a little leaf of escarole sloshing around in a plate—*nothing*. But we make the nothing into something. And then we project it out and it becomes some *thing*. It is material. It is real. It is reified. It becomes something that I can touch, I can smell, I can taste, I can hear, I can see and I can attack—*very serious!*

When you take anything in this world seriously, it means you give it power to change you. I was so calm and peaceful and gentle and soft, and all of a sudden this happened. It is not my fault. Something, someone out there did this to me. That is what you have to realize. Change it into soup and everybody is in the same soup—*everybody*. We are in the same miserable bowl of soup. We believe we are here. And there is no "there." There is only here. Heaven is now a forgotten dream, and the reality is this world, this body. And so we try to make sense of it. Therefore, it becomes very, very serious.

Seriousness versus the Gentle Smile

Whenever you take anything seriously, you know that is your ego. Do not forget that line: "Into eternity, where all is one, there crept a tiny, mad idea, at which the Son of God remembered not to laugh" (T-27.VIII.6:2). And then it goes on, "in its seriousness, did that idea become possible of both accomplishment and real effects." When we called it sin, we said it actually happened and was serious, we believed it happened; it was accomplished and had very real effects. What are those real effects? You and me, the world. The seeming reality of the world seems to prove that the thought of separation, the tiny, mad idea, was a fact: a sinful fact, a serious fact.

I frequently say that it is very important not to confuse the Jesus of the Bible with the Jesus of the Course. There is one very easy way to realize why that is so. Nowhere in the Bible—nowhere—does it ever say Jesus smiled or laughed. Read it carefully. It never says that. Throughout the Course, Jesus talks about the gentle laughter, smiling. He does not say giggling or tickling, but I think that is not too far off the mark.

The problem was not the tiny, mad idea. The problem is not expressing the tiny, mad idea in hatred and cruelty. The problem is that I forgot to laugh at it. I made it serious. What does it mean to make it serious? It means it has effects. That is what it means to make something serious. It has effects.

When I take something you do or something I hear about on the news or something that goes on in my body or the body of a loved one, and it changes me and I am now angry; I am wrathful, I am depressed, I am anxious, I am frightened, and I am not myself anymore, then I am saying what you have done has had an effect on me. That is what makes you a sinner. Sins have effects. The world is the effect of sin. You would not have a world if there were not the belief in sin. The world was made to escape from sin. But how could you escape from what never happened?

That gentle smile tells you nothing happened. That is what it means in the workbook when it says you will smile at sickness, starvation, poverty, suffering and death (W-pI.187.6:4). That is what it says, almost literally. Now that is a right-minded smile. That is not a derisive smile. It is not a dismissive smile. It is not an insensitive smile. It is a smile that says the thought system underlying this (which in that lesson is sacrifice) is nothing.

There is no sacrifice. God was not sacrificed so I could live. Christ did not have to be crucified so I could exist. Heaven did not have to be destroyed so I could live in this world. There was no sacrifice. Nothing happened. What the Course refers to as the sacrifice of Oneness, it never happened. It is not *one or the other*. My happiness is not predicated on your loss. My being innocent and sinless does not mean that you have to be sinful. It is not *one or the other*. It is *together or not at all* (T-1.IV.D.12:8). We are all the same.

What goes on outside in the world of bodies can have no effect on my mind. It can have an effect on my body. As long as I identify as a body, of course it will have an effect. And once it has an effect, I am saying you have sinned. Or if it has a positive effect, if it gives me pleasure, then you become my special love object. Then I hold the sin in abeyance until I do not get my needs met anymore. And it says in one section, then the barricades are broken through, and the hate that was always there now shines forth—if you want to think of hatred shining (T-16.IV.4:10).

Forgiveness means what you have done has had no effect on me. As I mentioned earlier, you forgive your brother for what he has not done. He has not taken the peace of God from you. That is what it means to laugh at sickness, starvation, poverty and death. That is all of the body.

If I really want to be of help to other bodies, I have to know that I am a mind. Otherwise, I am no different from physicians before the germ theory was discovered, who would operate on patients and not wash their hands. That is unheard of these days, right? Well, nobody knew about germs. A physician did not care about what was on his or her hands. I guess in those years, it was probably mostly "his" hands. You are cutting open a patient to help him and you are re-infecting him.

But that is what we are all doing. We are re-infecting each other with the disease of separation that we now call sin that is reinforced by our guilt that leads to our fear of punishment that leads to our need to defend against the punishment. How do we defend against punishment? We sin some more, which makes us guilty, which makes us afraid of punishment. We go around and around, two concurrent cycles: the guilt/attack cycle and the attack/defense cycle (W-pI.153.3:2).

They reinforce each other. The guiltier I feel, the greater my need to project it out and attack, magically thinking that is how I get rid of my guilt. And once I attack, I believe I will be counterattacked, so I have to defend myself against your counterattack. I have to attack you back, which makes me feel guilty, which leads to my having to attack, which leads to my having to defend against counterattack. I go around and around and around. There is a wonderful workbook lesson about that. It talks about this circle surrounded by "bands of steel" (W-pI.153.3:2), that keeps us in prison—attack and defense. "In my defenselessness my safety lies." It is Lesson 153.

What gets transformed is not what is out there. It is not the relationships in your life. What gets transformed is your thinking. Just flip a switch. It is not a vegetable; it is soup. That is all you have to do. And if you really think of that example, you could not help but smile. Then where is your anger? You cannot smile and judge at the same time. You cannot smile and be angry at the same time. In this bowl of soup, everyone is swimming together. And it is the garlic in the soup that will heal them. [Laughter] Any good Italian knows it. And everyone is in that soup or else no one is in that soup.

You will know that you have asked the great Transformer of perception for help when everyone is included. And when you do not include everyone, you will recognize that is what you are doing and you will understand why you are doing it.

The Forgiven World

Let me read you a line where that passage appears. It is page 353 in the text. This is the section called "The Forgiven World." This is one of those beautiful sections on the real world. And I am going to read paragraph 5.

(T-17.II.5:1-2) The real world is attained simply by the complete forgiveness of the old, the world you see without forgiveness. [That is the transformation. You will perceive the world differently because you have changed what is in your mind. Here is the line.] **The great Transformer of perception** [that is the Holy Spirit] **will undertake with you the careful searching of the mind that made this world, and uncover to you the seeming reasons for your making it.**

That is another of those sentences, if you just read this sentence and nothing else in this course; you would be healed, because this has everything in it. Whenever you find yourself upset, for whatever reason, whether it is something relatively minor or something relatively major, quickly go within and ask the great Transformer of perception to search your mind that made this particular part of this particular world. Do not go metaphysical. Go with what is making your world right now—I am angry at you, or I am dependent on you, and I am angry because you did not meet my need. That is the world you are making right now. Remember, there is no past; there is no future. We are all dreaming right now. We are making up the world as we are seemingly living it.

Remember, there is no world (W-pI.132.6:2); there is no time. There is no body. If I am upset, it is because right at this moment, I have chosen the wrong teacher. I have chosen the teacher of anger, of guilt, of specialness. Why am I making up a world in which you attack me? Not that I am responsible for what you do. I am responsible for how I perceive what you do. Why am I making up a world in which I perceive you as attacking me? Because that is what my ego tells me to do because that is what will preserve my identity.

The fundamental ego purpose for everything in this world, why it made the world, why it causes us to be born into this world—the fundamental purpose behind all of this is to keep my ego intact, to preserve my existence and prove that the ego is right, and to blame other people for it. If you examine your life thoughtfully with sincerity, you will recognize that twofold purpose underlies everything you have ever done as an ego.

You preserve your identity as an individual—I exist, I was victimized, I was abused, I was unfairly treated. "I," "I," "I"—but it was not my fault. Somebody did this to me. Some thing did this to me. Something out there, a hurricane, a snow storm, a blizzard, a tsunami did it to me. The economy did it to me. The people in Washington did it to the economy that did it to me.

Search your mind carefully. That is what this means. The Holy Spirit will search your mind with you—a careful searching of your mind. And if you think back to the early workbook lessons, you will see how often Jesus talks about searching your mind. He is not talking about your brain. He is not talking about you as an individual person. He is talking about the mind that transcends bodies, transcends space, transcends time.

He will help you realize why you did it. He will "undertake with you the careful searching of [your] mind that made this world, and uncover to you the seeming reasons for your making it." It is "seeming" because nothing happened. Why am I making up and reliving over and over again my abuse, my victimization, my unfair treatment, whether it is at the hands of another person or my body that will gradually fail me as I grow older? Why am I making it up right now? For two reasons, which are really heads and tails of the same reason. I want to preserve my identity—"I," my separated identity—and blame someone, something else for it.

Be honest with yourself, as Jesus asks us earlier in the text (T-4.III.8:2). Be honest with him and realize that is what is in back of everything I do. I believe *I* am studying *A Course in Miracles*. Ha. You are obviously not studying it all that well, if you think *you* are studying it. Who is studying it? There is nobody out there.

And why are you studying it? You are studying it because you are so unhappy. Who is unhappy? You are unhappy because as a person you are unhappy? You are unhappy because your mind chose the teacher of unhappiness that very cleverly says the reason you are unhappy is not because you chose me, the teacher of unhappiness. You are unhappy because of all these people in your life. We all do that. Why else would you be born? Why would any right-minded, sane person choose to be born in a body and live in a body and defend the fact that that is reality? That is what this is saying. This one sentence says everything.

(T-17.II.5:2) The great Transformer of perception will undertake with you the careful searching of the mind that made this world, and uncover to you the seeming reasons for your making it.

I want this to be a serious world that contains within it serious sinners. I know they are serious sinners because they have done irreparable serious damage to me or my loved ones or my race or my religion or my country. Serious, serious, serious. Once again, that is how you know that *A Course in Miracles* and the Bible are mutually exclusive. The Bible is a very serious book. Nobody laughs in the Bible. The central event of the Bible, if you are a Christian, is the crucifixion. What Christian would ever tell you that that is not serious, not only for what happened to poor Jesus, but he saved the world? That is serious.

A Course in Miracles is not a serious book. It talks about laughter. It talks about a gentle smile. It talks about remembering to laugh. It is looking at the tiny, mad idea and saying, "Oh, my God, it is nothing." It is a little piece of escarole floating around on a plate. What is so terrible about that? And all of a sudden, I flip a switch and now it is delicious soup. Nothing external changes. What changes is how we look at it. That is the transformation. That is the transformed world.

We transform the world in our minds from guilt to holiness, from judgment to forgiveness, from the ego to the Holy Spirit. When that thought is transformed, the world will appear differently to us. We will look at the world differently. Our eyes will see the same thing that we had seen yesterday, before we had this transformation, but our attitude will be totally different. Our focus is never on the world, on what is outside. The focus is always on what is in our mind.

Let us finish paragraph 5. It is on page 353 in the text. We stopped with sentence 2, so sentence 3.

(T-17.II.5:3) In the light of the real reason that He brings, as you follow Him [this is the Holy Spirit, of course]**, He will show you that there is no reason here at all.**

This is obviously a play on the word "reason," which becomes even more prominent a little bit later on in the text. Sentence 2 talks about how the Holy Spirit will uncover for us the seeming reasons for our making the world. But then in sentence 3, he talks about reason in the sense of logic. In the Course, the word "reason" (except when it has to do with cause—the reason I do something is, or something like that) is a synonym for right-minded thinking.

There is an important section later on, "Reason and the Forms of Error" (T-22.III). Again, reason in the Course is usually a synonym for right-minded thinking. And that is what it is talking about here. "In the light of the real reason that He brings," which really is a play on the word, where in a sense you have both meanings. The real reason for our making the world, which means the right-minded reason, is that it becomes a classroom.

There is a wrong-minded reason for my being born and making up the world that I seem to exist in as I go along. And the ego reason as I was saying before, is to preserve our individual existence and blame other people for it. But the right-minded reason for my being born into this world is that I will make all the ego mistakes until the point comes when I say, as Bill did that fateful afternoon, "There must be another way." And then the world becomes a classroom. Instead of being a prison, in which I suffer and try to blame other people for my suffering, it now becomes a classroom in which I learn that there is no world. That is the ultimate lesson.

The world becomes a means of recognizing which teacher I chose. The ego works from "inside outside." Jesus and the Holy Spirit work from the "outside inside." Going from the "inside outside" is projection. I make guilt real in my mind, and I attempt to get rid of it by projecting it out. Forgiveness or the miracle starts where we have ended up as egos. Instead of continuing to project going from the mind to the body, I now use my experiences as a body in the world as a means of gaining access to my mind.

Since I do not know I have a mind, let alone a decision-making mind, I need to monitor my perceptions and my feelings and my reactions. When they are anything but all-inclusive and all-loving and kind, then I realize I have chosen my ego. That begins the process of shifting my emphasis from my body to my mind, from the dream figure that I call myself, interacting with other dream figures, bodies; I now begin to realize I am the dreamer.

There is a line in Chapter 27, "*You* are the dreamer of the world of dreams" (T-27.VII.13:1). You are the mind that is dreaming of a world and bodies, with a past, a present and a future, a mind that is asleep dreaming of life as a body; dreaming of existence within a linear framework where there is a past held in place by my memories. There is a present, what I experience now, and a future that I anticipate.

The whole thrust of this course, which is why it is called *A Course in Miracles*, is that the miracle takes us from outside where the ego put us via projection and brings us back inside. I begin to realize the reason I am never upset for the reason I think is that I think I am upset because there is something going on around me, when the real reason I am upset is that my mind chose the wrong teacher. Pure and simple. So:

(T-17.II.5:3) In the light of the real reason that He brings...

The Holy Spirit brings us reason in the sense of right-minded thinking—not insanity. He also gives us a reason for being here—not to prove the separation real and blame others for it, but to ultimately prove that there is no separation. The purpose of time is to show us there is no time. The purpose of the world is to show us there is no world. There is an inner world. And it is that inner world that is the determiner of what I perceive outside. So once again, what I want to transform is not what is outside, but what is inside.

(T-17.II.5:3) In the light of the real reason that He brings, as you follow Him, He will show you that there is no reason here at all.

Meaning nothing here makes sense. There is nothing logical here. As I have said many other times, do not believe anybody who tells you two plus two equals four, because that is the reasoning of the world; that is the logic of the world where things seem to make sense. There is a cause and there is an effect. There are systems of rules and laws that hold. The fact of the matter is, if there is no world here, how could there be laws that hold? How could there be rules? How could there be principles that govern life here? The only principle that governs our life here is guilt.

The right answer is two and two is five, which means nothing here makes any sense. That is what is implicit in this idea that the Holy Spirit shows us that there is no reason here at all. Do not try to make sense of this world. It cannot be made sense of.

In Chapter 23 in "The Laws of Chaos" section, which gives a very in-depth and sophisticated summary of the entirety of the ego thought system, the introductory paragraph to that section talks about, these are the laws that govern the world that we live in, but you cannot understand them because they are not laws. In fact "laws" is put in quotes (T-23.II.1:1). They are seeming laws. But you can understand the purpose that they serve, which is to keep us rooted in the world of illusion.

What keeps us rooted in the world of illusion, as we saw earlier, is seriousness. We take the world seriously. Bodies are serious things. Serious things happen to bodies. Bodies do serious things to other bodies, all of which makes this world real. And if this world is perceived and experienced as real, the thought system that made it must be real, too, which is the thought system of guilt.

At the beginning of Chapter 13 is the line, "The world you see is the delusional system of those made mad by guilt" (T-13.in.2:2). That is what the world is. It is a delusional system, which means it is a thought system in the mind that is projected out. And it is made by those who are made insane by guilt. It is not the world you want to change. The world is not the problem. You want to change the thought system that made the world. You want to transform it from guilt to forgiveness. That is what this is saying.

(T-17.II.5:3-4) In the light of the real reason that He brings [the sanity, the logic of the two plus two equals five world, not the two plus two equals four world]**, as you follow Him, He will show you that there is no reason here at all. Each spot His reason touches grows alive with beauty, and what seemed ugly in the darkness of your lack of reason is suddenly released to loveliness.**

Now if you take this literally, reading it as a body, you will actually believe as you forgive, the world will become beautiful. The deserts will bloom. Disease will be no more. That is not what this is saying. Everything in this world will be touched by the beauty of your mind, which means you will see everything in this world and everyone in this world either as expressing love or calling for love. That is the only thing you would perceive.

It is really important that you not get caught in that level confusion that Chapter 2 talks about, which is the confusion of mind and body. That is why I keep encouraging everybody to always remember, even if it is not your experience, that this is not about the body. This is not about the world. This is not about changing the world through *A Course in Miracles*. And once again, how could you change a world that does not exist? Insane people think like that. Delusional people who hallucinate think that way.

Everything we perceive in this world through the eyes of reason becomes a classroom that reflects back to us, as the introduction to Chapter 21 says, "The world you see is an outside picture of an inward condition" (T-21.in.1:5). It is an outside picture; it is a projection. Lesson 23 says the same content: "The world is a pictorial representation"—a pictorial representation (W-pI.23.3:2). It is a projection. It is an outside picture. It is not real. You want to change your thinking. You want to change what is underneath it. You want to change the source of your perception, not your perception itself in terms of objects.

(T-17.II.5:4) Each spot His reason touches grows alive with beauty, and what seemed ugly in the darkness of your lack of reason is suddenly released to loveliness.

This will be transformed in your understanding and your reading when you recognize he is talking about the beauty of the real world in your mind, which means you will look out through an extension of that inner beauty and you will have no attack thoughts at all. You will look at sickness, starvation, poverty and death and you will not be trapped in the form. And you will realize that underneath all of them is the belief in sacrifice: *one or the other*. And that belief is of the wrong-minded thought system of the ego.

You want to represent the right-minded thought system that says *together or not at all* (T-19.IV.D.12:8). And even though we appear to be different by our forms—you are suffering and I am not, or I am suffering and you are not, or this group is suffering and this other group is not—underlying all the forms is the same content. We all suffer from the same sickness, from the same disease of guilt. Guilt is a decision. Guilt is a decision that we made to push away the innocence of God's Son that we did not make.

In the section called "The Two Emotions," Jesus says "...you have but two emotions, love and fear. One you made and one was given you" (T-13.V.10:1). The one we made, of course, in that context, is fear or guilt or sin. The other was given to us in our creation. Guilt is not a natural state. It is something we made up. Guilt is a decision, just as anger is a decision, fear is a decision, sickness is a decision, death is a decision, birth is a decision. And it is a decision of the mind.

That is why it is imperative that you realize, again, this is about the mind, not the body. Otherwise, you will read a passage like I just read to you, and you will be very angry and disappointed when all of a sudden, the world has not changed. You turn on the news and it is still about famine and disease and murder and bombs and rape and death and hatred and torture. And you will say, "Well, he lied to me." Well, he did not lie to you, because you did not remember his line, "Nothing so blinding as perception of form" (T-22.III.6:7). As I was saying earlier, form is just another word for specifics.

Give me your blessing, holy son of God.

Lesson 161, which talks about specifics, refers to God as Divine Abstraction (T-4.VII.5:4). That is who we truly are. We are part of Divine Abstraction. Actually, it does not use that phrase there. It uses that in Chapter 4 of the text.

(W-pI.161.2:1-2) Complete abstraction is the natural condition of the mind. But part of it is now unnatural.

The part that is unnatural is the ego. The part that is natural is the right mind that contains the memory of divine abstraction, which is nonspecific. That is why I always emphasize that Jesus and the Holy Spirit do not do things in the world, because the world is a place of specifics. They do not guide you to do specific things. They do not give you specific functions or missions.

Remember, there is no hierarchy of illusions. Teaching *A Course in Miracles* is no different from being a plumber or a teacher or a parent or an athlete or a government official. They are all the same because the mind is the same. You do not want to do anything that reinforces separation or fragmentation or specialness. That does not mean people do not do different things. But that is just an opportunity for realizing we may do different things, but we have the same mind; not only because all minds ultimately are one, but because we all have the same split mind. That is what unites us. You do not want to choose to make real or significant anything that divides us or separates us out one from the other.

You know, as I have often said, that is why Helen would never encourage people to make her special. She would say, "What I have done, you could do." It is always the same voice. Do not ask me to do something for you, like have Jesus tell you what to do, when you can do it for yourself. She would invite people to pray with her so they would hear the same voice that she was hearing, because it is one voice. It is very tempting to make people special, to say there is a hierarchy of people. There is a hierarchy of holiness—holy places, holy objects, holy books, holy people, holy clothing, holy food, holy rivers, holy walls. It misses the whole point: *Nothing so blinding as perception of form.*

The Forgiven World (cont.)

Back to "The Forgiven World," this is the end of paragraph five.

(T-17.II.5:5) Not even what the Son of God made in insanity could be without a hidden spark of beauty that gentleness could release.

What we made in insanity is the world. And again, the world is a "dry and dusty world where starved and thirsty creatures come to die" (W-pII.13.5:1). It is a place of disease, deterioration, death, pain, cruelty, war, etc., etc. But even that has a hidden spark of beauty. Why? Because everyone has a right mind. Take the worst serial killer you can think of, take the worst dictator or head of state you can imagine; there is a right mind there.

Since I have been telling Gloria stories, let me tell another one, which was an experience we had in Australia in 1984 when we were speaking there. This was in the height of what the United States was doing in Central America, and all the terrible regimes we (USA) were promoting. Right outside where we were speaking during the lunch break, there was a park with a whole group of people protesting American policy in Central America, and Gloria was right in the midst of that.

We came back and began the afternoon workshop with a meditation. While she is meditating, having led everybody in a meditation, she is quiet, and she suddenly sees Ronald Reagan, who was not her favorite person, and she sees light all around him. That was very disconcerting to her at the time. Then she shared all this with the group. Ronald Reagan, who for her was the embodiment of evil for the policies he was promoting—even he had that spark of beauty in him and had that light.

Everybody has a right mind. *Everyone has a right mind.* Take your favorite criminal, your favorite villain; even that person has a right mind. Take the person in your personal life, the one in your personal life whom you hate more than any other, that person has a right mind, too. And all the darkness that they may be spewing forth is their plaintive plea, their call for help, "Please show me I am wrong." Now it may not seem the direct way to ask for help, but that is all they can do because they are so gripped in the horror of their own guilt and self-hatred and the insanity of it that all they can do is just spew it forth in this maladaptive, magical attempt to get rid of it by attacking other people.

Most of you are familiar with the line in Lesson 134, whenever you are tempted to accuse anyone of anything, ask yourself, "Would I accuse myself of doing this?" (W-pI.1 34. 9:3) When you call someone less than human, when politicians call their enemies dirty names, when nation states call the people they are at war with dirty names, when you call people in your life, in your family, in your workplace dirty names, and you think of them as less than human, you can only be doing that because that is what you believe about yourself.

If there is any emotional investment in anything you say about anyone else, it must be a projection—*if there is an emotional investment*. That does not mean, therefore, that if you are watching the news and there is a story about a serial killer at loose, that you are a serial killer. But if you get angry, if you get judgmental, if you get frightened, then that has to be a projection. It has to be, because if you were right-minded, you would not be angry. You would not be judging. You would not be calling this person a dirty name. You would not be seeking vengeance.

That does not mean you let serial killers or rapists run loose. But if you stop them, you stop them not because you are afraid or you are angry, but because you are stopping them from harming other people and stopping them from harming themselves through what they are doing. Remember, when you kiss someone who is sick, you either get their germs or you bring them your health. It is the same activity. It just depends where you start from.

If you have any emotional investment in any judgment that you make, you know it has to be your ego. Because if you are right-minded, you will be calm, you will be gentle, you will be caring, you will be kind, and you will be loving. And that kindness and love would embrace everyone. That is what this is saying—"without a hidden spark of beauty that gentleness could release." Gentleness, kindness, being loving, being thoughtful—they are all the same.

When you ask help of the Teacher of kindness, you must be kind to everyone, because *projection makes perception*. What is within you must be projecting out. If it is only kindness, then you must see everyone through kindly eyes.

I frequently quote that wonderful little stanza of William Blake. He talks about vision and judgment, even though he does not use those words. He says that you do not see when you look with the eyes instead of through the eyes. And what he is talking about is when you look with the eyes, you are seeing form and you are judging and you will be blind. When you look through the eyes, he is talking about vision, without using those words. In that same stanza, he talks about how the senses do not let you see. Almost two hundred years before the Course, he was talking about *nothing so blinding as perception of form*.

The "Spark of Beauty"

Everyone has a right mind. Everyone has a spark of beauty. Everyone, including all of us, is terrified of that spark of beauty. Because if we look at the spark of beauty, that hint of Atonement, that Thought that says the separation never happened, that spark will quickly catch fire and embrace us in its warmth and its light. And in that embrace, our specialness would cease to exist. And eventually, our individuality would cease to exist.

We are all doing what the serial killer, what the rapist, what the bomber is doing—all of us. Not in the same form. But we are all trying to deny that spark of beauty. We are all trying to deny that light and that truth that is in all of us.

And if it is not in all of us, it is in none of us. That is the part of the Course that is, without question, the most difficult to practice. *Together or not at all* (T-19.IV.D.12:8). Right at the end of the text in that glorious final vision of Jesus, he says: "Not one spot of darkness still remains to hide the face of Christ from anyone" (T-31.VIII.12:5). The face of Christ is the Course's symbol for innocence. *Not one spot of darkness still remains to hide the face of Christ from anyone.* Not one. That spark of beauty is in everyone or it is in no one, including Jesus or any other enlightened figure you can think of.

What defines the Sonship is its wholeness. What defines the Sonship of Christ is its perfect wholeness, in which there is no differentiation, no fragmentation. When Jesus talks about the Holy Trinity—Father, Son and Holy Spirit—he says there is no Holy Trinity (T-14.IV.1:8). God is first in the Trinity, and there is no second and there is no third. We speak of a Trinity; we speak of a differentiation within the Godhead because differentiation is our reality. Therefore, Heaven is presented as differentiated.

He says that in the section called "The Link to Truth" (T-25.I). Heaven is presented as separated and differentiated because that is what we think we are. That is the condition in which we think we exist. The language is that. But God is First; and there is no second and no third (T-14.IV.1:8). There is only God. There is only the perfect wholeness of the Godhead. Creator and created do not exist in Heaven because you do not have two. Father and Son do not exist. Cause and effect do not exist. There is only One.

I sometimes talk about Plotinus, who was the great 3rd Century Neoplatonist, which means he was a follower of Plato. He was absolutely wonderful and he was not religious. He lived in Rome and he taught in Rome, which obviously was very, very Christian, but he was not Christian. When he referred to the Absolute, he referred to it as the One. That was the word that came the closest that he could use because there are no words to depict this—the One. We say we are all part of the One, but there is no part. We have the illusion of being a part. Since we are apart, we think we are *a part*. But wholeness does not have parts.

In fact, near the beginning of the text, Jesus contradicts one of the basic theorems of geometry that says the whole is equal to the sum of its parts. He says the whole is greater than the sum of its parts (T-2.VII.6:3). What makes Christ Christ, is not that you add up all the fragments like a pie, and you put it back together again like Humpty Dumpty. There are no parts. The whole is greater than the sum of its parts. If you absent one person from the Sonship by virtue of your judgment, you are saying there is no Sonship. You are saying fragmentation is the rule, differentiation is the rule, and separation is the rule.

This does not mean you should feel guilty. It just means do not justify your judgments. I always like to point out that there are two places in the Course where Jesus says the same thing: Anger is never justified (T-30.VI.1:1; M-17.8:6). But he never says do not get angry. We are all angry. Only angry people come here because you have to do something with your guilt. The guilt is intolerable so you have to project it out. But he says do not justify it. He is not saying do not have specialness; just do not justify it.

In fact, he has that line where he says, I am not telling you to see your brother as sinless, because I know you cannot. I am asking you to *want* to see him sinless. Do I really wish to see my brother sinless? (T-20.VII.9:2) That is the thing. Do I really wish to? This is a process. We are not asked to let go of a thought system that is our foundation; that is our DNA, and that is the warp and woof of our existence. He is not asking us to let that go.

He is asking us to question it. Do I really wish to see him sinless? Do I really wish to see myself sinless? It is the same question. If I am sinless, I am not guilty. If I am not guilty, I am not sinful. If I am not sinful, I am not separated, which means I do not exist. We need to perpetuate the lie about sin and guilt. And we preserve the lie by projecting it out, making a body, making the body real and making other bodies the repository of our projected guilt, which we now forget we have done. It is a brilliant, brilliant plan.

So again, this sentence is saying:

(T-17.II.5:5) Not even what the Son of God made in insanity [or cruelty or hatred] **could be without a hidden spark of beauty that gentleness could release.**

That is why it is so important not to see yourself as a body, and to realize this course is leading you to be a mind, because it makes no sense otherwise. Bodies do not do nice things. People do cruel things. Animals do cruel things to each other. Look at plants; look at trees fighting for survival. Look at what their roots do underneath, strangling other roots so that they would get the water.

Everything here is cannibalistic. Everything here is vicious, as bodies, because bodies cannot survive without taking from some other body. We cannot make our own food. We cannot manufacture our own oxygen. We have to take it from outside. We have to take water from outside. We have to take nutrition from outside. And on a psychological level, we have to take love from outside because we do not believe we have love.

There is no hope if we are bodies. The hope only lies in realizing we are minds. Minds do not have needs. The only need the mind has is the need to remember that it is a capital "M" Mind. That is the only need the mind has. Everything else is nonexistent.

The transformed world is the transformation in our perception that sees everyone has this spark of beauty—*everyone*. And it will be revealed to me when I am gentle, when I do not attack, when I do not judge, when I am kind. It always boils down to the same thing. Just be kind. It is like Jesus saying over and over again, "Please be kind."

Do you not realize what you are doing when you are being unkind? Even unkind in thought. When you judge one person, only one person; when you get angry at bacteria: what is the difference? If you say, well, it is only bacteria. It is going to invade me. It is going to hurt me. You are saying there is a hierarchy of illusions. You are saying that bacteria do not have a hidden spark of beauty.

The mind is not homo sapiens. Sorry. God is not a member of homo sapiens. Do not be taken in by forms. *Nothing so blinding as perception of form.* What is transformed is not the form. What is transformed is our perception of the form.

The Forgiven World **(cont.)**

Let us look a little bit further, paragraph 6.

(T-17.II.6) All this beauty will rise to bless your sight as you look upon the world with forgiving eyes. For forgiveness literally transforms vision [literally transforms vision], **and lets you see the real world reaching quietly and gently across chaos, removing all illusions that had twisted your perception and fixed it on the past. The smallest leaf becomes a thing of wonder, and a blade of grass a sign of God's perfection.**

This is not pantheism. This does not mean God created a blade of grass. There is no blade of grass. When you realize that you are perfection, that you are a sign of God's perfection, everything out here will be perfect, even if the eyes judge it as imperfect because your right mind will look right past the wrong mind to the other person's right mind and see the call for help. And see the answer to that call not in you, not in them; in everyone. It is the same call for help. It is the same answer.

Now in truth, there is no ego and there is no Holy Spirit. These are personifications of a thought of guilt and separation or a thought of forgiveness and healing. There is no separated ego any more than there is a separated Holy Spirit. We are the ego. We are the Holy Spirit. We just give them names and objectify them so it makes it easier for us, as long as we think we are separated, to relate to them.

In fact, near the beginning of the Course, Jesus apologizes in one passage for his talking about the ego as if it were a separate thing. But, he says, I have to do this. For pedagogical reasons, I have to teach like this. Because you think that there is something outside of you affecting you. So I give it a name. I call it the ego. But it is not a separate thing. You are the ego. As long as you want to be separated, you are the ego. And as long as you say, there must be another way, there has to be something more than this—that is the Holy Spirit.

As you begin to realize more and more that you are not a body, you are not a person and you are not a separated entity, the ego and the Holy Spirit will fall away as separated categories and as separated experiences and as separated persons. And you will realize they are symbols. They are symbols of me when I am insane and symbols of me when I am sane. And at the end, you will realize the inner voice you are hearing is your voice. But it is not the voice of separation, it is not the voice of specialness, it is not the voice of your ego.

There is only one voice. There is only one Voice in Heaven and there is only one voice in the illusion. We have the illusion of two voices. When we choose the one Voice that undoes the ego voice, then that one Voice of the Holy Spirit disappears, too (C-6.5:8). In the clarification of terms, the section on the Holy Spirit says that. It says the Holy Spirit is an illusion, but it is a necessary illusion because we think we are an illusion that is trapped. We need the illusion of help that reaches into the morass of guilt that we know as this world and lifts us out of it. We are too afraid to realize the power of our minds to choose one or the other.

As long as we are afraid of the power of our minds, that power is given away to the ego or the Holy Spirit. In the end, however, as we ascend the ladder and get closer and closer to the top of the ladder, which is the real world, we will realize more and more it is one Voice. It is me. I am the ego; I am the Holy Spirit. I am the ego; I am Jesus. There are no separated symbols. They are only there to be separate as long as I think I am separated.

What lets this whole thing change for us is forgiveness. That is the gentleness. And then everything will be perceived, will be experienced as God's Son. In another passage, Jesus talks about, you will realize even the smallest grain of sand is part of God's Son (T-28.IV.9:4). Now that makes no sense in a two plus two equals four world. But it makes every sense when you recognize that form is irrelevant. There is no hierarchy of illusions. Form is always illusory. Everything in this world that has form, that has substance, whether we think it is alive or not, animate or inanimate, is a projection of the wrong-minded thought system, the *tiny, mad idea* taken seriously, which means it becomes capable of real effects, which is the world of materiality, the phenomenal universe.

What is helpful on a practical level is to realize that I cannot change what is out there, but I can change what is in me. You want to shift your focus from the world. The world does not need transforming. It needs forgiving. And when you forgive the world, you are saying, the world I see is not out there. It is an "outward picture of an inward condition" (T-21.in.1:5).

It is my mind that chose guilt that has to be forgiven by me. When you are forgiving towards me and nonjudgmental, you are showing me the other way. As the manual says at one point, you stand for the Alternative—capital "A" (M-5.III.2:6). It says in that same paragraph, it is not what you say; it is not what you do. It is the Presence that you represent. It is in the function of a teacher of God in the teacher's manual.

Let us skip to paragraph 8. And this is the crux of the problem.

(T-17.II.8) How much do you want salvation? [That is the issue. How much do you want it?] **It will give you the real world, trembling with readiness to be given you. The eagerness of the Holy Spirit to give you this is so intense He**

would not wait, although He waits in patience. Meet His patience with your impatience at delay in meeting Him. Go out in gladness to meet with your Redeemer, and walk with Him in trust out of this world, and into the real world of beauty and forgiveness.

How much do you want salvation? That is the question to ask yourself each and every moment. And when you get angry, when you indulge your fantasies of specialness, when you feel despairing, when you feel anxious, when you feel afraid, when you think anything in this world is meaningful and important to you, you are saying I am not ready yet. I do not want salvation.

In the workbook, it is said twice: Why wait for Heaven? (W-pI.131.6:1; 188.1:1) Well, we have a very good reason for waiting for Heaven. I like who I am. Even when I am miserable and I look in the mirror and I hate myself, there is a self that I hate. I like that. From the point of the ego, it does not matter whether God loves you or hates you. He notices you. It does not matter how terrible I feel about myself. As long as there is a self that I relate to, I am happy—maybe not consciously. Why do I dream a dream in which I am miserable? To fulfill the ego's purpose. I exist; somebody else did it to me. That is why people love to talk about their past—*love* to talk about their past.

I have been writing to a prisoner who writes volumes to me. And his volumes are all about his past. He is a student of the Course. He is a very bright guy. Yet he cannot stop writing about his past, even when I write back and say something and try and be cute. I still get volumes. I got another twelve pages today. It is all about his past. And yes, he has a pretty awful past, and a lot of awful things happened to him, and he probably is being treated very unfairly in prison, etc. But he will not let it go, because that is what defines him. That is why people do not let go of their childhood abuse.

We are all like the ancient Mariner in Coleridge's wonderful poem. I quote this every once in a while. We are all the ancient Mariner confessing our sin to everybody. He has to tell the story over and over again; how he shot the albatross, which is a symbol of innocence—it is a white bird. Because he is so guilty, he tells the story. Each time he tells it, it makes it more and more real. Even though he is pleading for forgiveness; he is compelled to tell the story.

We are compelled to tell our life story. What do you do when you meet a person for the first time or you are getting to know a person? You tell them your story. And I am not saying not to do that, but just be aware of what you are doing. You are defining yourself by your past. That is what egos do.

What if there were no past? What if you knew the world is an hallucination? Which is a literal question that Jesus asks (T-20.VIII.7:3). But what if you knew that there were no past? What would you talk about? Who would you be? Again, I am not saying not to do it. I am simply saying step back and think about it and look at it. Who would I be without my problems? Who would I be without my current problems, my past problems, my anticipated problems? And you must realize that you hold onto these. You cherish these.

I sometimes refer to that passage in the *Psychotherapy* pamphlet where Jesus talks about the "hugging-close" of guilt (P-2.VI.1:3). We just hug it close to us. That is why in "The Obstacles to Peace," Jesus talks about the attraction of guilt, the attraction of pain, the attraction of death—not the fear of it, *the attraction.* "The attraction of guilt" section is really about my being attracted to the guilt in you (T-19.IV.A.*i*). But the only reason I am attracted to the guilt in you is because it makes the guilt in me real—hidden, but real, because it is a projection. Who would I be without my stories?

But there is a reason for the stories. They fulfill the ego's two-fold purpose: I exist by virtue of my stories; but it is not my fault. Things happen to me. I am not minimizing people's pain. Awful things happen to children. But invariably the children that awful things happen to carry that with them, which tells you there is something rotten there.

I sometimes define memory—this is not in the Course, but it is certainly based on what the Course says—as a present decision projected into a nonexistent past. Memory is a present decision my mind makes right now that I then project into a nonexistent past. My present decision is for the ego and its thought system. I then deny that my mind chose that. I deny that I am a mind. I project it out, and I say the reason I am unhappy is not because I chose my ego. I am unhappy because of what happened to me when I was younger, or what my boss said to me yesterday, or what you said to me over breakfast this morning.

I am not aware that I am literally making it up. It is my dream. And there is a purpose behind it. It preserves my ego identity and makes other people responsible for it. I am seeing no beauty. I am seeing no hidden spark of beauty. I am seeing spots of darkness that I think are real. And I have all the evidence. I am like a lawyer. I bring to bear all the witnesses that will convince the jury that the defendant is guilty. I am a prosecutor, I am the defendant, I am the jury, I am the judge. And I want to prove myself guilty but then make somebody else responsible for it. That is what we do.

It is very helpful to step back and look and see what we do. We are asked in the Course to look back in honesty (T-30. V.10:1). Looking back in honesty means I am looking back at nothing. I am looking back at a projection of a world that does not exist, never existed, that I think exists. And I keep perpetuating it in my memory because it proves that the separation is real, I am real and somebody else did it.

Again, I am not minimizing people's pain, and I am certainly not saying you should deny it. I am saying; however, look at how you do not want to let it go. And you want to hold onto it as a defense against being a mind that is choosing right now to either be in a state of conflict or a state of peace. That is the bottom line.

"How Much Do You Want Salvation?"

How much do you want salvation? Are you willing to devote every single moment of every single day so that everything you do and think and say and feel is geared towards helping you awaken from the dream? That is the question you should ask yourself. And why not do that? As a sincere student of the Course, as you all are, why would you not devote your day to what this course is asking of you? "Choose me as your teacher," Jesus says, "so I can instruct you on how to look at your world differently. I could transform your vision." And then realize your resistance, your fear of doing that.

That is what it means to look with honesty. It is realizing I do not want to let this go because I am afraid of letting me go. Remember the line I quoted to you at the beginning today. The Holy Spirit does not take away your special relationships (T-17.IV.2:3). He does not take away your special relationship with yourself. He transforms it. He changes its purpose. You do not go from nightmares to reality. It is a gentle process in which the nightmares become happy dreams and eventually lead you to awakening to reality.

The transformation of yourself is not a total transcending of yourself, just like that, because we are too afraid of "just like that." We need, to use a phrase from the manual, a "slowly evolving training program" where we gradually begin to see what we are doing (M-9.1:7). Just to quote to you that line again from the previous page, paragraph 5 on page 353:

(T-17.II.5:2) The great Transformer of perception will undertake with you the careful searching of the mind that made this world, and uncover to you the seeming reasons for your making it.

Making it right now. Why am I choosing right now to hold onto the past? Why am I choosing right now to be angry, to be anxious, to be fearful, to be excited about something? Why am I choosing it right now? That is what he is uncovering. Not why did I make up the world as part of the collective Son, seemingly fifteen billion years ago? Someone sent me an article today that said scientists now say it is thirteen point seven billion years ago, plus or minus a few hundred thousand years.

He is uncovering the reasons for my making it right now, as I am sitting here in this room—*right now* when I am *not* focused on what will lead me to the acceptance of the Atonement. I am focusing about how my body feels right now or how dinner will taste or how the people will feel whom I am having dinner with, or whatever. If your mind is not absolutely focused on what we are speaking about, it is because you are afraid of the implications of accepting the Atonement.

So your mind wanders. Why do you think I have to say the same thing over and over again for thirty-five years? Why do you think this book says the same thing over and over again? Because people's minds wander. That is not a cause for judgment or for guilt. It is a cause for realizing, "Yes, I am really afraid." That is what this is saying again.

He will help us uncover "the seeming reasons for your making" this world. And think very specifically about your very specific world, the world of your thoughts right now, the world of your relationships and your job and the state of your body. That is the question to ask all the time. *How much do I want salvation?* And if I really want it, I will devote every waking moment, not to mention my sleeping moments—every moment towards leading me towards acceptance of the Atonement.

And if I do not do that, I have no one to blame but myself. *Expose the lie of projection.* Projection says someone is responsible for this. The only one responsible for anything that you experience or feel is your decision-making mind.

If you wanted to state succinctly what the purpose of the Course is, it is to get us back in touch with our decision-making minds. That is why the book is called *A Course in Miracles* and not *A Course in Love*. Because: the miracle is the Course's name for the process of leading us from our perception of a world out there to the inner perception of being a mind.

On a very practical level, that is what you want to look at. How much do you want salvation? You all know, I am sure, from your past experience, that when you had a real specific goal, you attained it. And everything had to be set aside so you would attain it. Anybody who has ever written a doctoral dissertation knows you do not get it done unless a period of time comes when you devote twenty-four hours a day to it. You eat, drink, and sleep it. Otherwise, it does not get done. Because that is important to you, you do it.

I remember when my first marriage ended, and I found myself for the first time in my life in debt. I was never in debt before except when I paid back a car loan. And I did not like it. I remember the next year; I counted every single penny I had. I did not have a high-paying job at that point. I really counted every penny. I watched my electric bill and my phone bill and the gas I put in my car, etc., etc. Because: I wanted to get out of debt. It took me a whole year and I finally did it. I was single-minded, because that was important to me. And everybody has had examples of that.

Why don't you do it for the most important thing in your life? What could be more important to you than to be saved from your guilt and to awaken from this dream? This does not mean you should feel guilty when your mind wanders to all objects of specialness—special love or special hate. But just be aware of what you are doing. *Get to the content behind the form.*

The Laws of Chaos

Let me read to you from "The Laws of Chaos," page 489 in the text, paragraph 1. Now this is the introduction to this very long and brutally graphic discussion of these five laws of chaos and then what follows from them.

(T-23.II.1) The "laws" of chaos can be brought to light, though never understood. Chaotic laws are hardly meaningful, and therefore out of reason's sphere. [You cannot understand them.] **Yet they appear to be an obstacle to reason and to truth. Let us, then, look upon them calmly** [which means gently, kindly, non-judgmentally], **that we may look beyond them, understanding what they are, not what they would maintain. It is essential it be understood what they are for, because it is their purpose to make meaningless, and to attack the truth. Here are the laws that rule the world you made. And yet they govern nothing, and need not be broken; merely looked upon and gone beyond.**

And what you look upon is what they are for. When you find your mind wandering to thoughts of specialness, feelings of specialness, acts of specialness, look beyond the form and say, "What is this for?" What it is for is to hide that hidden spark of beauty, to keep it hidden. It is to keep you rooted in the dream because you are so afraid of awakening from it. It is saying, "I do not want salvation."

In other words, be honest. *Be honest.* Jesus says at the beginning, "Be honest with yourself...we must hide nothing from each other" (T-4.III.8:2). Not that he would hide anything, of course. Be honest. Let me show you through my gentle non-judgmental light the purpose behind all your specialness, all your attachment to specifics, all your being bored, all your being tired, all your being angry, all your being anxious, fearful, all your reading the Course and falling asleep. I will not mention people sleeping here. That may be right-minded thinking.

There is a purpose behind it. You are a student of this course, and you are a sincere student of this course and many of you for many, many years. Obviously, this is important to you, but not that important. That is what you want to look at. You do not get out of debt unless you really work towards it. You do not get a dissertation completed unless you really work for it. You do not get an important exam passed unless you focus on it night and day. And you will not achieve salvation, you will not accept the Atonement unless it becomes your only purpose in life. That is what you have to see.

How much do you want salvation? Why wait for Heaven? Enlightenment is a constant state. It is there. It is not off in the distant future. It is right here. It is in your mind. And if you are afraid of transforming your mind to be right-minded instead of wrong-minded, you will make yourself mindless, which, of course, is the ego's consummate strategy. If I am mindless, if I am a body, I do not know I have a mind, so how could I change it? How could I transform my perception when perception has nothing to do with the world but only with the mind? How can I ask help of the great Transformer of perception if I do not know I have a mind?

That is the purpose behind being a body. *Think purpose.* Everything has a purpose. Every thought you have is purposive. Every feeling you have, whether you think it is a natural feeling of the body or an emotion—a psychological thought—everything is of the mind. There are no natural laws of the body like hunger or sleep or sex or the need for protection from the elements. These are not natural. There are no bodily laws. How can what does not exist have a law?

That is why Jesus pokes fun at all this in Lesson 76, "I am under no laws but God's." Here he pokes fun at the laws of nutrition, the laws of immunization, laws of relationship, friendship. Again, this does not mean you should feel guilty about adhering to bodily laws, to eating, etc. It does mean at least look at the purpose that they serve. That is all.

Just to go back to what I just read in "The Laws of Chaos"—page 489:

(T-23.II.1:6-7) Here are the laws that rule the world you made. And yet they govern nothing, and need not be broken;...

They need not be fought against. You do not have to struggle with these laws. You merely look upon them and go beyond. And you do it calmly. When Jesus says the same thing at the beginning of "The 'Dynamics' of the Ego" section in Chapter 11, he uses the same word, "calmly." He says "Together we have the lamp that will dispel the ego." *Together*—it means we have to join with him.

And he says we will look calmly beyond them. We will look at them so we go beyond them. We are calmly looking for the truth. We are doing this calmly, gently, patiently, kindly, sweetly, quietly, softly. You do not press forward on this. If you do, you are pressing forward because you think it is real, which means it will never work. You do not struggle with this.

That is why I plead with you, "Do not take the Course seriously." Because then you are going to struggle with it. You are going to try to make salvation happen. How could you make it happen? It has already happened. You just have to look. But you cannot see because there are all these veils—these veils of guilt that get projected into form. So you want to look at these veils and say, "I now understand the purpose they serve, and I recognize I am not ready yet to let them go." But at least now I know why I am not letting them go. I am preserving this individual self. I would much rather spend time transforming the world than transforming my mind.

Where Sin Has Left

Turn now to page 549 in the text. This is the other section I mentioned, which is very, very beautiful in depicting what the real world is. It is called "Where Sin Has Left," which actually really goes to the heart of what the process is, and actually what we are going to read in paragraph 4 on page 549. Where sin has left is the state of the mind where there is no sin. If there is no sin, there is no separation; there is no guilt, there is no projection, there is no fear. There is only the Atonement.

All we are asked to do is to look at the ego without judging it. We are asked to look at the ego and remember to laugh at the silliness of even having entertained the thought there could be anything other than God, let alone wanting there to be something other than God. When we look calmly with Jesus' loving light beside us, and we look at the illusions and we recognize their purpose and finally say, "I do not want this anymore," they are gone. All the illusions are gone and where sin has left now arises this beauty of the real world. But paragraph 4 helps us look more at the process.

(T-26.IV.4:1-3) Forgiveness brings no little miracles to lay before the gate of Heaven. [There are no little miracles; there are no big miracles, because they are all the same.] **Here the Son of God Himself comes to receive each gift that brings him nearer to his home. Not one is lost** [not one gift is lost]**, and none is cherished more than any other.**

This is because there is no hierarchy of illusions. Not one gift is lost, meaning not one experience in this world, not one perception of anything in the world of form is lost, and none is cherished more than any other. That is the end of specialness. "None is cherished more than any other" because everyone is seen as the same. The forms are different, but they reflect the unity of the split mind, the inherent sameness of the split mind, despite the myriad number of forms.

(T-26.IV.4:4) Each [one] **reminds him of his Father's Love as surely as the rest.**

Why? Because everything out here leads us back within. And when I go back within my mind, I can choose again. And I can choose my Father's Love instead of the ego's hate.

(T-26.IV.4:5-6) And each one teaches him that what he feared he loves the most. What but a miracle could change his mind [meaning transform his mind]**, so that he understands that love cannot be feared?**

I fear love because in the presence of love, I do not exist. So I am cherishing this illusory self. How absurd is that? I am cherishing a self that does not exist.

(T-26.IV.4:7-8) What other miracle is there but this? And what else need there be to make the space between you disappear?

Meaning: between you and your brother. What is important about this paragraph is that it really is saying the way out of hell is to bring the illusion to the truth—*every illusion*. If you think back to the early workbook lessons, one of the salient principles that underlay these early lessons is Jesus saying, "Do not exclude anything." As your eyes go around the room, nothing in this room means anything (W-pI.1). Do not exclude anything. Now that does not mean you have to include everything, because you cannot. In the two or three minutes allotted for that exercise, you cannot include everything. But do not purposefully or deliberately exclude anything.

In this world, you cannot love everyone in the world of form. But you can let go of the need to love certain special people and not others. Forms differ for our love obviously. But behind the forms, there is the same love, which is born of the recognition that we are all the same. That is the key thing. We are all the same. We need to practice with each one. Just see how many times this appears—"each gift," "not one is lost," "each reminds him," "each one teaches." You cannot exclude any lesson.

Now you could exclude it and say, "Well, I am not ready to do this." That is honest. But do not make up stories why you are not doing it. Remember, again, what I was saying earlier: the most difficult part of this course in practice is its non-exclusivity and all-inclusivity. Everyone must be included in your forgiveness.

To make the point again, if there is not a spark of beauty in this one person, it is in nobody. And if I see a spark of beauty in one person, it must be in everybody. That is what is so difficult, because our lives are built on differentiation, on good guys and bad guys, *one or the other*, special love, special hate. That is what has been learned and overlearned and overlearned and overlearned. It takes a lot of discipline, twenty-four hours a day. How much do you want salvation?

Well, the right answer in terms of what most people's experience is, "I do not want it now." Most of you may know the famous prayer of St. Augustine, who before his conversion was not a very nice man, especially when it came to the opposite sex. His prayer was, "Lord, make me chaste, but not today." "Lord, make me chaste, but not today." Well, that is what we say to Jesus in this course. Make me happy, but not quite. Help me to forgive everyone, but not today. And of course, we mean not tomorrow, either.

It is very important to be honest with yourself and recognize what you are doing. We are not asked to let go of our egos. We are simply asked to look at the ego, recognize its purpose, recognize why we are still holding onto its thought system and realize this will not bring me the peace of God. And in my insanity at this moment, I prefer the peace of the ego, which means I get what I want, rather than to have the peace of God, a peace that is inclusive of all people, all situations, all events, all everything—all objects, all animals, all plants, all minerals—everything. I am kind to everyone and everything because I remember, as the workbook says, *"Kindness created me kind"* (W-pI.67.2:4).

If I want to remember God and who I am as God's loving extension, I must be like Him. Kindness created me kind. Which means: when I am unkind in word, thought or deed, it is because I do not want to remember my Creator, pure and simple. That is all you have to do. If the memory of God comes to a quiet mind, when my mind is not quiet, that is a decision. When I find myself ruminating over things and plotting revenge or mourning my terrible fate, it is purposive. It keeps my mind in a perpetual state of disquiet so the memory of God will not come to me. Because when the memory of God comes, I exit. And that is not what I want to do.

It is very helpful, if my mind is to be transformed, that I recognize how much I do not want the transformation. That is the beginning, because that is what undoes the resistance. And just be honest. Remember, we are not asked to become *Course in Miracles*' saints. We are just asked to want to be. Just as we are asked, "Do I really wish to see my brother sinless?" Do I really wish that I be sinless? And it is not a sin to say: "No, I don't want to see myself sinless, yet." And if you can be kind and gentle with your resistance, it will cease to be resistance.

Closing: "Transformation"

I want to close by reading one of Helen's poems, "Transformation," which actually I have read other times. But it is perfect for our topic today. There is a story in back of it. Let me tell it briefly. I have told it other times, and it is in my book on Helen, *Absence from Felicity*. The story is important only because it sets the stage for what the poem talks about, which then can become a model for what our lives ought to be day in and day out.

This occurred on Palm Sunday, which was also, it happened, the second day of Passover. Helen and I went down to two very dear friends of ours who were Maryknoll Sisters who lived on the Lower East Side (Manhattan), with our good friend, Father Benedict. We used to call him Father Michael in the old days to protect his identity because he did not want to be associated with the Course, but since he has written books about it now, I will just call him by his name. Benedict was the only priest I have ever known who said Mass as if he meant it. I am not saying he is the only priest out there, but the only priest that we had known who said Mass as if he meant it. He was very close to us and to these Sisters.

He had thought since Palm Sunday was also the second day of Passover that I should do a Passover Seder. I did that and we had a meal. Helen had written a poem a couple of weeks earlier called, "The Place of Resurrection," which is a lovely Easter poem. I forget who read it, whether Helen read or I read it. Probably I did; Helen did not like to do those things. So I read that at the end of the meal, and then we were going to go into the chapel and Benedict was going to say Mass.

I read the poem and it is a very beautiful poem. As I finished it, there was a stunning silence that just happened. Nobody said a word for minutes. And it was a moment outside of time and space. On the way home, Helen and I were talking about this because it was a very remarkable and stunning experience. And I said to her, as was my fashion, this would make a great poem. So the next morning, she presented me with this poem. It is a lovely poem that really talks about the transformation of perception. Just let me read you a couple of lines that I will read when I read you the poem ("Transformation," *The Gifts of God*, p. 64).

> The trivial
> Enlarge in magnitude, while what seemed large
> Resumes the littleness that is its due.
> The dim grow bright, and what was bright before
> Flickers and fades and finally is gone.

In other words, what shifts now is what we thought was so important, namely that the world and world of bodies begins to fade into nothingness. And what we had judged as not important, which was the mind, all of a sudden now becomes much more important. That is the transformation. The world is perceived differently because the mind has now been transformed. And that is what this poem represents.

Since it was written on Palm Sunday, it closes with an Easter reference. It says: "Be you free, and stay not here. Go on to Galilee," which would be a symbol of the resurrection. In other words, do not stay in the place of crucifixion. Go now to the place of resurrection, and that, of course, would be the complete transformation.

Transformation

It happens suddenly. There is a Voice
That speaks one Word, and everything is changed.

You understand an ancient parable
That seemed to be obscure. And yet it meant
Exactly what it said. The trivial
Enlarge in magnitude, while what seemed large
Resumes the littleness that is its due.
The dim grow bright, and what was bright before
Flickers and fades and finally is gone.
All things assume the role that was assigned
Before time was, in ancient harmony
That sings of Heaven in compelling tones
Which wipe away the doubting and the care
All other roles convey. For certainty
Must be of God.

It happens suddenly,
And all things change. The rhythm of the world
Shifts into concert. What was harsh before
And seemed to speak of death now sings of life,
And joins the chorus to eternity.
Eyes that were blind begin to see, and ears
Long deaf to melody begin to hear.
Into the sudden stillness is reborn
The ancient singing of creation's song,
Long silenced but remembered. By the tomb
The angel stands in shining hopefulness
To give salvation's message: "Be you free,
And stay not here. Go on to Galilee."

The Ego's World: "The Thunder of the Meaningless"

Introduction

The title of the class is "The Ego's World: 'The Thunder of the Meaningless,'" which is a nice phrase from workbook Lesson 106 (W-pI.106.2:1). This is another way of talking about what we *always* talk about; the inherent nothingness of the ego. Since "Ideas leave not their source" (T-26.VII.4:7), and "Projection makes perception" (T-13.V.3:5, T-21.in.1:1), if the thought of the ego is meaningless, then the world that arises from it must be meaningless. When we talk about the "ego's world," we are talking about both the wrong-minded thought system, which obviously is in the mind, as well as the physical world that appears to arise from it.

Both are equally meaningless; however both equally make a lot of noise. That is why it is such a lovely phrase, "the thunder of the meaningless." It makes a lot of noise by simply saying: "I exist, here I am, I am real and I am awful." The ego comes into seeming existence by virtue of the belief in sin, which is a pretty awful thought, that gives rise to the equally horrifying experience of guilt, and that leads to the fear of punishment, which is the worst of all. And then to escape from all that, we make up a world that we think is going to hide us from the wrath of God and protect us. We end up in a body that is as weak as can be, and yet makes a lot of noise. Bodies themselves make noise simply by the process of existing, and certainly we make a lot of noise in terms of what we do with each other. And it is all meaningless because it is all inherently nothing.

I thought I would start by just reading the beginning of Lesson 106, in which that phrase appears. What is helpful as you read it, and where Jesus talks about the inherent nothingness and meaninglessness of the ego and its world, is to consider what the implications of this are. And, of course, it is the implications of this that is what strikes the fear of God in us. Actually, it strikes the fear in us because what this is really saying is not only do we not count, and not only are our lives meaningless, but we do not even exist, and that is the bottom line. That is why we read words like this, and the passages I am going to read obviously are similar to everything else in the book. But they are terrifying because they point out the absolute nothingness of our existence, and the fact that we are always trying to make something of us.

The whole idea of specialness which, of course, is the ego's way of preserving its identity, is all about "Notice me, I am special, I am important." We make a lot of noise to have God and everybody else look at us and notice us. A passage I frequently refer to from "The Fear of Redemption" section in the text talks about how we asked *special favor* of God, and He did not give it to us. He did not give it to us because He *could* not give it to us.

The *special favor* we wanted from God was that He notice us; that He notice we exist independently of Him (T-13.III.10:1-4), to see us as a separated, differentiated being. God could not notice us. He could not grant us that special favor because we are not separate from Him. So we then made a lot of noise! That is what sin, guilt and fear are. That is what the ego's self is. That is what the world ends up being. We make a lot of noise saying to God, "Notice me." And, of course, God does not even know anything about this.

One of the readings that you have is "The Little Garden," in which it talks about how we are like a little ray of the sun and a little droplet on the water, and that the ocean and the sun do not even know about us. We are like an infinitesimal ripple, and we keep thinking we exist and yet the ocean does not even know about us. The sun does not even know about this little ray (T-18.VIII.3-4). That is the bottom line of why we are so angry at God, because He does not notice us. He does not know that we are gone. To us, of course, that gets interpreted as that He does not *care* about us. Well, of course, He does not care about *us* because there is no "us" to care about. But *that* is what is so frightening.

I have sometimes said over the years, you will know you are making progress with this course when the idea that God does not know about you makes you happy, *really happy,* because that is your ticket home! That is salvation, because if He noticed you, there would be a "you" to notice, and then you are hopelessly stuck in this prison with no way out. The only way out is to realize the whole thing is an illusion. Our individual lives, along with the cosmos in which our individual lives seem to exist, is the *thunder of the meaningless*. It is nothing. It is not only the thunder of the meaningless; it is the thunder of the *nothingness*.

But you must at some point recognize that this is all about saying, "The person I think I am, not only is not important; ultimately it is not even here. God does not know about me." If you pay real attention to that and think about, it would have to strike *tremendous* anxiety, terror, panic in you. "Because: if God does not know about me, and God is the only reality and the only truth, then I am not here." So then we make even more thunder and more noise.

That is what our problems are, that is what our abuse stories are, victimization stories, our rejection stories, our pleasure stories, our happiness stories; they are all about thunder. "Notice me! I make noise. I am important. I am significant. I have a holy function. I have a holy mission. I am a holy person." Or equally: "I am an *un*holy person. I am a miserable sinner." It does not matter as long as "I" exist.

That is what we really hold against God. He does not know about us. It would be fine if He knew about our sin and punished us. That is why the Bible is such an incredibly popular book. God notices us. There is that line at the end of a very important specialness section in Chapter 24 that ends by saying, "Forgive your Father it was not His Will that you be crucified" (T-24.III.8:13). "Forgive your Father it was not His Will that you be crucified." What we will *never* forgive God for is that He *does not* want to punish us because He does not see our sin.

We are very comfortable with a god who crucifies. We are very comfortable with a savior like Jesus who wants us to suffer and sacrifice the way *he* suffered and sacrificed. We are *not* comfortable with a savior who says there is nothing to be saved *from*. Nothing happened on the cross because there is no cross. There is nothing to be sacrificed. There is nothing to be sacrificed *for* because nothing happened. We are uncomfortable with a God Who says, "What are you upset about? Nothing happened. You are still at home in God, dreaming of exile" (T-10.I.2:1).

What we cannot forgive God for is that He *does not* want to crucify us. He does not want to punish us because, "If He punished me, He *noticed* me." I would prefer that He like me and notice me. But if I do not have a choice, I would rather He notice me and punish me than He not notice me at all, because I could always strike a deal with Him if He is going to punish me.

That is what religions do. They strike a deal with God. We will be good boys and girls. We will do this; we will do that. We will obey your commandments and your laws and your rituals. This is all across the board; any formal religion, East or West. It is striking a bargain with God: "Do not punish me. Don't kill me. I am sorry. I did a bad thing. I will never do it again. I promise. And I will devote the rest of my life to you." It is a bargain, as if God makes bargains.

That is another example of the *thunder of the meaningless*. Theology is meaningless. Theories of salvation are meaningless because there is nothing to be saved from. But it is a lot of noise, it is a lot of words, it is a lot of concepts, it is a lot of behavior. That is our fear, that we would look in the mirror and suddenly realize that all the thunder of our lives; all the *Sturm und Drang* of our special relationships, the ups and the downs, all the angst of our lives, all the ecstasies of our lives are simply the thunder of the meaningless. That is what you should try to think about as I am reading to you now. But when you read this on your own, just think of how your individual life applies to this, and then try to apply these words to your individual life.

Let me be still and listen to the truth.

We will start at the beginning of Lesson 106.

(W-pI.106.1) If you will lay aside the ego's voice, however loudly it may seem to call; if you will not accept its petty gifts that give you nothing that you really want; if you will listen with an open mind, that has not told you what salvation is; then you will hear the mighty Voice of truth, quiet in power, strong in stillness, and completely certain in Its messages.

What is implied in this paragraph is the very important theme of *purpose*. We *do not* want to hear the Voice of truth, because the Voice of truth is the Voice of the Atonement that says *nothing happened*. In order *not* to hear the Voice of truth, we listen to the ego's voice. And so the egos of the world tell us what salvation is. They write books about it, all of which constitute the thunder of the meaningless. And then we *listen* to them and we follow them. We feel guilty when we do not follow the principles of salvation. And then we have this exalted sense of holiness when we *do* follow them.

But it is all designed to silence that still, small Voice that speaks of truth; that *is* the truth, because that is what we are afraid of. If the Atonement is true, then the separation never happened; *I* never happened. I mean it is *very* simple. You understand that, and then everything in this course will be crystal clear because everything in this world is designed, everything of the body, everything of specialness, everything of what the world calls "spirituality and religion" is designed to silence the still, small Voice of truth that says *nothing*. It does not have theories of salvation. It simply smiles sweetly at the thought that we could be separate from our Creator. That is what this is saying.

(W-pI.106.2) Listen, and hear your Father speak to you through His appointed Voice, which silences the thunder of the meaningless, and shows the way to peace to those who cannot see. Be still today and listen to the truth. [Which is the title of the lesson. "Be still today," which means be still to the voice of the ego. Be still to any voice that speaks of separation, differentiation or anything that makes the physical world real and the body real. "Be still today and listen to the truth."] **Be not deceived by voices of the dead, which tell you they have found the source of life and offer it to you for your belief. Attend them not, but listen to the truth.**

Many of you have heard me say often: "Do not believe anyone that tells you two and two is four because they are among the voices of the dead." They are telling you there is a logic in this world; you can make sense out of this world. How can you make sense of the meaningless? How can you make sense of what never happened? All the laws of this world, all the mathematical principles and theorems, all the scientific "truths" are designed to make the error real, to make us believe there is a world out here that follows certain principles. In fact, some people will tell you the world is *divine* and follows a divine principle: that all is as it should be, always. All that is done to make the underlying *thought* real; which is that separation is the reality and perfect Oneness is the illusion.

If we could show that this world is real and follows laws, laws that hold and are true, then it means the underlying *thought* is true, which means my personal existence is true. Anytime anybody says anything to you that comes from a premise, explicit or implicit, that says the world is real, the body is real, there is a hierarchy of illusions, there is a hierarchy of spiritual practice, there is a hierarchy of people, there is a hierarchy of jobs, there is a hierarchy of places and objects, etcetera; *do not listen.* That is what this is saying:

(W-pI.106.2:3) Be not deceived by voices of the dead, which tell you they have found the source of life and offer it to you for your belief.

That is what all the "two plus two equals four" brains of the world have done from the beginning of recorded history, from beyond and from past recorded history. Anyone who tells you they have figured it out, whether they are chemists, biologists, physicists, astrophysicists, psychologists, doctors, teachers, *Course in Miracles'* teachers; when they tell you, "I have figured it out," what have they figured out? That two and two is *four*? They have figured out *nothing*. They have analyzed the thunder of the meaningless, and have come up with what they believe are cogent theories, and they are all wrong. That is what this is saying. They are all designed *not* to hear the still, small Voice that speaks truth and only truth; that says nothing here is real. Everything here, *everything* here is an illusion that is designed to perpetuate the *thought* of illusion.

That is what is *so* frightening. What is so frightening about a lesson like this, and every other lesson and every other section in the text and manual, is that they all reflect that same basic truth: *nothing happened.* On a practical level, this means that before you could be involved in the world (and there is nothing in this course that says you should not be doing things in the world), before you could be involved in this world, you first have to realize there is no world that you are involved in. And before you are ready to fully accept that truth, at least you could recognize there is nothing in this world that I really value. "The world I see holds nothing that I want" (W-pI.128). That is a later workbook lesson.

It does not mean not to be involved in the world. It just means do not make it salvation. Do not make it Heaven, do not make it hell. The world is not the problem. The world is not the answer. If you really want to be effective in this world and you truly want to be helpful, you could only be truly helpful and effective in this world if you know there is nothing here that you want and need, which would then be the stepping stone to awakening one morning and saying there is nothing here at all. This is not only the thunder of the meaningless; it is the thunder of the *nothingness*.

The very beginning of the workbook is that way. Nothing in this world has any meaning. Nothing in this room has any meaning (W-pI.1). The early lessons are all about that. Everything is meaningless. They are meaningless because we have given them meaning, whether it be a relationship, whether it be a religion, whether it be an object, whether it be a coffee cup. We have given everything its meaning. That is why it is meaningless.

Learning the Meaninglessness of the World

The only meaning in this world is learning that there is no meaning here. As you learn that more and more by not giving anything in the world power over you—power to make you happy or power to make you unhappy—as you do that more and more, one day it will dawn on you, "There is nothing here." But before you get to that point, you must first recognize "There is nothing here that I want," which always gets us back to the tyranny of needs.

Once we are separated, there is this sense of lack and scarcity in us and we always need to fill it, just as we always need to fill our bodies with food, water and oxygen. We also need to fill our psychological bodies with respect and love and attention and sensitivity. We want people to be caring and thoughtful, approving. We always have to fill up the lack. That is the need. That generates this whole hierarchy and tyranny of needs that is the heart of the special relationship. I need special things from special people, from special objects; otherwise, I cannot exist, physically and/or psychologically.

The whole thing is meaningless. The only thing we need is to realize we have no needs. The text says, "The only meaningful prayer is for forgiveness" because you have everything (T-3.V.6:3). Forgiveness is what awakens us from the nightmare and the seeming reality of the ego and its world saying, "There is nothing here. I just have to remember this is an illusion!" Everything here is the thunder of the meaningless.

We are not asked to skip steps, we are not asked to skip over things. Before we know there is nothing here in this world (it is totally an illusion, totally a dream and nothing else), we first live within the dream, live within the illusion, but without giving it power. That: we could learn how to do. That is what the process of forgiveness is. You do not deny your experiences in this world. You do not make-believe there is no pain and suffering, there is no death; there is no this, there is no that. You do not make-believe that that does not exist because you believe it does, because you think you are a body. But you begin the process by learning that nothing can hurt me, which leads us to probably the most important theme of all, which occurs over and over and over again in the Course: *that we are not bodies, we are minds*.

As I was saying previously, and I think I say it in every class, you will not understand this course and you will not practice it correctly if you do not understand, at least intellectually, that you are not a body. That is why that is such a salient theme throughout. The sentence that appears more than any other in the workbook is: "I am not a body. I am free" (W-pI.rVI.in.3:3-5). It is the basis of a 20-day review period, as well as various lessons. "I am as God created me" (W-pI.rVI.in.3:5), which is spirit, not a body. Again, we are not asked to deny our bodies, but we are asked to deny the *meaningfulness* of our bodies and other bodies in our lives.

Remember, very, very simply, the criterion to use to evaluate any experience you have: "Does it make the body real? Does it make the world of specifics real? Does it make separation and differentiation real? Does it reinforce those perceptions?" And if it does, you know it is the ego. But when your experiences here become part of the classroom of learning that we are not different and we are all the same, then you will learn that bodies in and of themselves are meaningless. What people say and think and do with me or say and think about me is meaningless!

The only thing that is meaningful is what *I* think about me. Am I child of the ego, or am I a child of God? Am I a pupil of the ego, or am I a pupil of the Holy Spirit or Jesus? The *only* thing that is important is what *I* think about me. Once I think and remember Whom my real Teacher is and Whom my real Creator is, then if people say unkind things about me, I do not take it personally. Unkind things can only be said from an ego about an ego; from a body to a body; from a person to a person. True kindness is from a mind extending itself to embrace other minds. The experience is mediated through bodies because that is what we think we are, but it all has its source in the mind, "Ideas leave not their source" (T-26.VII.4:7). That is the criterion.

In the lesson a little bit after this, "I will not value what is valueless," Jesus says the one criterion to use to evaluate and distinguish between what is valuable and what is valueless is: "Does it last? If it does not last, it has no value" (W-pI.133.6). Well, kindness in the mind lasts, forgiveness in the mind lasts, as long as you think there is a dream and there is a split mind. Everything else makes bodies real. Which means for example: if you are only kind to a specific person, who is in a specific circumstance that is *kindness-to-destroy*. If it is true kindness, it may be aimed at a certain person in a particular situation, but it does not exclude anybody and embraces everyone.

Now it is certainly true that when you are unkind, it also embraces everyone. But the unkindness reinforces separation, because the basis of unkindness in any way, shape or form is to say, "I am innocent and you are guilty; therefore, you do not deserve my kindness." True kindness recognizes we are the same. The ego's form of kindness or its outright attacks are always saying we are *different*. "You are the sinner, you are the one who should feel guilty, you are the one God would punish." Since it is *one or the other*, if He punishes you, I am off the hook.

The Purpose for Listening to "the Thunder of the Meaningless": Mind versus Body

Any act that you do, any thought that you have that makes bodies real, to be loved or to be hated, whether it is your own or anyone else's, is an expression of the voice of the dead. Once again, that is why you should not listen to anyone who believes two and two is four. Anytime anybody gives you any advice, or you read an article, or watch a news program, or pick up the phone, or write a letter—ask the question: "How much is two and two?" If they say, "Four," shut the set off; close the newspaper, delete the file from your computer because they will lead you wrong. They will lead you astray. They will lead you into the *meaningless* and they will tell you, "It is meaningful because I have a theory that proves it. I have a theorem that demonstrates it. I have a principle that always holds. It is *true*."

They will simply lead you further and further and more deeply into the meaningless; that is the *thunder of the meaningless*. It is all purposive (albeit unconsciously so). It is all purposive to keep us from hearing that "mighty Voice of truth, quiet in power, strong in stillness, and completely certain in Its messages" (W-pI.106.1).

What you need to do is to *really* listen. Before you could listen to the Voice of the Holy Spirit, to the Voice of truth, to the Voice of kindness, you first have to recognize how you are listening all the time to the voices of the dead, the voices of the meaningless. Without judging yourself, without calling yourself dirty names, simply say, "I am afraid. I am afraid of the simple truth, and so I make everything very, very complicated."

There is a line in the text that says, "Complexity is of the ego" (T-15.IV.6:2). The various forms of the *thunder of the meaningless* in the world are very complicated because they are all trying to explain an illusion. The simple thing to do with an illusion is say it is an illusion. Then the only meaningful question is, "Why am I continuing to believe in the illusion and trying to substantiate it in my experience?"

You need to *watch* yourself. Again, without judging, watch yourself and say, "Yes, I am doing it again. I am listening to the voices of the dead." You cannot stop listening to the voices of the dead if you believe that you are a body, at least as a student of the Course. Recognize that that is the problem, even when you still identify yourself as a body, even when you still have the insane thought that there is a "you" reading a book called *A Course in Miracles*. That is an insane thought. There is no you. There is no body.

Bodies do not see, they do not hear, they do not think, they do not hold a book, they do not have hands to hold a book. They do not do anything. They are part of the voices of the dead. They are part of the world of the dead that perpetuates the illusion that you are a body. That is how the ego uses the Course and takes the language of the Course, which is designed to meet us where we think we are, and it says: "Ah, this proves that we are here! It proves that there is a Jesus. It proves there is a Holy Spirit. He tells me what to do in the world. He tells me I should forgive my brother. That means there is a 'brother' out there. The book says it!"

Sure, the book says it. But the book *lies* if you read it as truth. That is why Jesus says the Course comes in an ego framework (C-in.3:1). That is why he tells us words are but symbols of symbols, therefore, they are "twice removed from reality" (M-21.1:9-10). Now we would call this a "white lie" because its purpose is to heal, not to hurt. But it is a lie. It is not literally true. How could it be true that I have to forgive you when Jesus tells me there is no "you" to forgive? There is no world out there (W-pI.132.6:2).

I am not saying not to believe the Course. I am saying go beyond the Course's *symbols* to what it is really teaching. You cannot do this as a body. You could only do it by realizing all this is about a mind. The Course is a symbol of my right-minded thinking. Jesus is a symbol of a right-minded presence that I think is not me. I am really a mind, but I *think* I am a body. Understanding that and saying things like that to yourself will help break that almost absolute identification with the body and the thought system of the ego that made the body.

Again, I am not suggesting at all that you deny your body. I am simply saying, step back and recognize what the body is and give it a different purpose. Instead of the ego's purpose of solidifying the dream, use it as a means of learning that, "This *is* a dream, and my reality is outside of the dream." You must *want* to learn that you are a mind reading a book that is your own right mind. You must want that to be your ultimate experience. Otherwise, you are stuck with just one more special relationship, and all three books and an entire curriculum whose express purpose is to undo specialness will become the vehicle of reinforcing specialness.

That is why all formal religions, regardless of their inspirational source, end up reinforcing specialness. That is why there is that line in the *Psychotherapy* pamphlet that is in the section, "The Place of Religion in Psychotherapy," where Jesus says: "Formal religion has no place in psychotherapy; but it [also] has no…place in religion" (P-2.II.2:1). Once you formalize something, you make it real, and then you worship the *forms* instead of what the forms should reflect, which is the content.

Jesus tells us the special relationship is a triumph of form over content (T-16.V.12:2). The implicit context of that section is Christianity. It is a triumph of form over content. That is what religion does. It takes the content of pure teaching—a non-ego teaching coming from love—and turns it into specialness. You could see that certainly in Christianity. What went wrong right at the beginning is: guess who was made special? Right off the bat you know two and two is four. Run like hell the other way.

The authors of the Bible did not believe that there was no hierarchy of illusions (T-23.II.2:3). They believed some people were better than others. Even the Jesus in the gospels believed some people, some groups were better than others. Read it carefully. You will see the prejudices because it is all about specialness. Those are the voices of the dead. Those are the *thunders of the meaningless*. Anything that differentiates and makes the differentiations important, significant, and real, do not believe them. "Attend them not, but listen to the truth" (W-pI.106.2:4). Do not listen to the voices that tell you, once again, two and two is four; that God can be figured out, that we could understand what salvation is.

Most of you know the line in the text: you still believe "your understanding is a powerful contribution to the truth, and makes it what it is" (T-18.IV.7:5). All theologies are an attempt to understand what cannot be understood and then make it real. You still believe *your* understanding is necessary for the truth and makes it real. This goes not only for theologies; it goes for *all* "isms," all ways of understanding, all theories of any kind, no matter what the discipline. It is an attempt to say, "My understanding is important," without realizing that it is my understanding that makes it seem real, which means it is *my* truth. It is the ego's truth.

You must really question everything that you think, especially about *A Course in Miracles*. People think, "Oh, there is a plan here." How could you possibly know what the plan of *A Course in Miracles* is? That is the arrogance of the ego; that is the thunder of the meaningless that is trying to take the Course and fit it into a two plus two equals four world.

Everybody swears that they know what is going to happen on 2012, one year away. That is the arrogance. That is trying to fit into a conceptual scheme the idea the brain understands a world of time and space when there *is* no world of time and space. That is why Jesus refers to this kind of thinking as "senseless musings" (W-pI.139.8:5). And basically says, sometimes very explicitly, but other times implicitly, there is no way of understanding this so let us talk about what you *can* understand, which is learning how to forgive.

Forgiving is not doing anything *positive*. It is undoing what is negative. You do not have to understand why two and two is five, but you *do* have to understand that two and two is not four. There is a big difference. You do not have to understand what "two and two equals five" means. You do not have to know that there is a mind, experientially. But you *do* have to know that two and two is not four and that the body is not where it is at.

That is what the early workbook lessons are about. I have always said that people tend to dismiss those early lessons as being a little simplistic and a little boring and, "Let's get onto the really good stuff." Well, the whole Course is found in those early lessons. The entire non-dualistic metaphysics of *A Course in Miracles* is found in those early lessons. They are not simplistic at all. They are *simple*, but that is where the profundity is found. Profundity is not found in the complex. It is found in the very simple.

Learning Not to Believe "the Voices of the Dead"

Do not attend the voices of the dead. Do not believe them. Do not listen to them. Even as you have to live in a world of two plus two equals four, learn how to do that. It is very, very important to learn how to live in a two plus two equals four world. Just do not believe it, which means you do not take it seriously, which means you do not give it power to affect you. Just think about all the things that affect you; all the things: big things, little things. A person does not smile at you the way he or she used to or should smile at you, and your whole world is shattered. A person says an unkind thing and you go into bouts of depression. You look at the stock market figures and there is a little number that you do not like, and all of a sudden, anxiety comes, or a little number that you do like and you are euphoric.

The most trivial thing in the world—a mark on a piece of paper that you think symbolizes something—throws you into the heights of ecstasy or the depths of despair. An expression on a person's face, an innuendo in a voice lifts you up or drags you down. That is how little we think of ourselves, that we are so weak and puny the slightest thing outside can make our day or destroy our day. All this is true if you are a body. All this is true in a two plus two equals four world.

It will have no effect on you if you are with Jesus above the battleground, if you know that you are a mind, if you know you are the *dreamer*, not the dream. The miracle establishes that you dream a dream (you dream a dream, meaning you are the dreamer), and the content of the dream: separation, differentiation, judgment, attack, the content of the dream is not true (T-28.II.7:1). All we are asked to do is to follow the pathway of the miracle, to have Jesus be our teacher and to explain to us that all we need to do is not believe the lies. That is all. Just do not believe the lie.

You do not have to know the truth. You do not have to have this wonderful experience of the truth with heavens opening up. All you have to know is "*do not believe the lie*." What is the lie? Anything that is of time and space. Anything that is predicated on the principle two and two is four and things here make sense. Anything that makes the body real: anything that differentiates you from other people or differentiates certain special people, either in your personal world or the world at large, from other people. That is part of the lie. Do not believe it.

Again, you do not have to accept the truth because at this point that is too frightening. As I was saying at the beginning, the truth is "not one of us is here." But you do not have to accept that. What you do need to accept is that the world lies to you. People who have it all together and will explain it to you are lying to you and that goes for *A Course in Miracles* too. The truths are not in this book. The truths are in the right mind that is the *source* of this book. We give it a name. We give it the name "Jesus." We give the name "Helen" to the person who brought this forth. But if there is no differentiation and we are all the same, *we* wrote the Course; not as bodies, not as personalities, but as the one right mind.

A Course in Miracles is only one expression of that right mind. It is an expression of the right-minded thinking of the Atonement principle that a whole group of people can accept. But there are thousands upon thousands of *other* expressions of right-minded thinking, as the Course itself says (M-1.4:1-2). And those would be for people who will relate to those sets of symbols rather than *A Course in Miracles*, which is one particular set of symbols. It does not make this set of symbols better or worse than any other. It simply means it is a set of symbols that I relate to, which may not be what you relate to, but it does not matter. The form does not matter.

I know Course students get very upset by seeing the same thing happening with the Course as happens with any religion. People fight with each other, they argue with each other, they criticize each other, they form schisms, they form groups, they form cliques, and they are upset that this is happening. I have always told people, "Why are you so upset? What did you expect? For thirty-five years it has been happening with the Course, and it will happen for another three thousand five hundred. That is what people do.

What does that have to do with you? What does that have to do with you and *your* work with this course? If it bothers you, then you are not working with this course correctly, because you are giving something outside, power over you. "I want something in this world that is pure. I want something in this world that people do not screw up." Well, if you want something pure, *go back home* because you will not find it here. Which is why we left home, because it was *pure*. There was no room for even the slightest spot of darkness in Heaven.

Once you are here, you are already saying, "I believe in impurity. That is my home; all these spots of darkness. And I will take any expression of love, and I will drag it through the mud of my spots of darkness." What is so surprising about that? We will make special relationships out of *anything* and anyone, including *A Course in Miracles* or any other expression of right-minded truth. What is the big deal? If it bothers you, then realize you are saying two and two is four. "I know what is needed in this world. It is *A Course in Miracles* unadulterated, pure, without schisms, without arguments, without hatreds." And you do not realize that this is a setup. Your ego is setting you up.

That is why I always say to people, *A Course in Miracles* is written for one person: *you*. You do not have a sacred mission. You do not have a holy function. It is only for one person: *you*. When you fulfill your function of accepting the Atonement, you will realize that you, the one person, is not the name you gave yourself. It is the one Son of God. That is what frees you from being mired in the throes of specialness, which always differentiates—*always*. It makes *you* special, makes your work special, makes other people special, makes *A Course in Miracles* itself special.

That does not happen if you know you are a mind and you understand *A Course in Miracles* is just one form, or expression of the right-minded thought system of Atonement. That is so *freeing*. Then you do not get caught in all the specialness. Then what people do in the world of bodies with it will not bother you! What people do with *you* will not bother you. If it bothers you, it is because you think you are a body and you demand that spirituality be expressed in a body in your particular way, and it will never happen—*never*.

You are just setting yourself up, and there is an underlying purpose in that. It is because if I could prove that the Course does not do what it says or that people screw it up in the world, then what good is it? I do not have to bother with it. Just one more example of what the ugly, cruel, evil world does with purity and truth, which means you forgot to read the first page of "Self-Concept versus Self" in Chapter 31, which talks about the "face of innocence." It is section V in Chapter 31 (T-31.V.2:6).

The face of innocence never makes the first assault, but the world is always imposing on it and impinging on it. That is what you do as a student of the Course when you let yourself get upset by all the wars going on and the battles and the judgments and the hatreds and the specialness, because you are reading it as a body, thinking there are other bodies out there. There *are not* any other bodies out there. This is all in the mind. Do not reinforce the dream.

Lift yourself *above* the battleground of the dream and remember you are a dreamer. On the level of the dreamer, there is only *one* decision you have to make: "Do I choose for my ego or do I choose for the Holy Spirit?" That is it. Do I choose for the teacher of differentiation and the significance of differences? Or do I choose the Teacher of *sameness*? If you choose the Teacher of sameness, what seems to go on in the world of form (what the Hindus call the *world of multiplicity*) will not affect you, because you will see every expression, everything in this world through the Holy Spirit's eyes as either an expression of love or a call for love. That is all it is and there is nothing else. It simplifies your life. It makes your life so, so, so much easier.

At any moment that you have a slight twinge of anxiety or judgment or anger or hurt, you could quickly realize: "I have done it again, and it is not what I as a person have done. My mind became afraid of love and chose the ego's version of love. That is what I believe protects me, so I can remain among the thunder of the meaningless, so I can remain as one of the voices of the dead." I, too, will preach the gospel of two plus two equals four, except I will do it in the name of spirituality. Which means I will believe *God* thinks two and two is four too, which means I could make sense out of this world. I could make sense out of the Course-world. I could make sense of why the Course is here and what its purpose is. It only has one purpose: to help *you* heal your mind. That is its purpose. Anything else makes the world of time and space real.

Sometimes people cite the statement Helen had made about the "celestial speed-up." And they use that as a way of justifying their belief that the Course is here to speed up people's Atonement path and get people home faster, etcetera. Unless they read my book, they would not realize Jesus never told her there was a celestial speed-up. The message Jesus gave Helen afterwards was that anything that makes time real, do not pay attention to, such as a celestial speed-up (*Absence from Felicity* page 181). It is a cute phrase that brings God into the world of time and space. That is why you should not believe it.

The only purpose of *A Course in Miracles* (and you will not understand it if you think you are a body), is to help you (the "you" being you who believe you are separated) heal your mind of that insane thought. That is it! Otherwise, you are just thundering meaningless thoughts and meaningless understandings. I frequently refer to those passages that say regardless of the subject, whether it is holiness or the miracle or forgiveness, your only job is to choose the miracle or choose to forgive. How these extend through you is not your responsibility.

Your only job is to accept the Atonement. That is right at the beginning of the text in Chapter 2. "*The sole responsibility of the miracle worker is to accept the Atonement for himself*" (T-2.V.5:1). It says it, and it says it *all* the way through in different forms; all three books, the pamphlets, *everything*. Your sole responsibility is to accept the Atonement for yourself; that is it. Not to change the world, not to heal the world, not to give brilliant lectures, or write esoteric books that nobody reads or understands. Your only job is to accept the Atonement for yourself, which means to realize you are a mind and not a body. What bodies do in this world is absolutely irrelevant. There is no world in which bodies could function.

Doing versus Undoing

The ego is the doer. God simply *is* (W-pI.169.5:4); perfect Being, perfect Love, perfect Oneness. He does not *do* anything. He *is*. The ego *does*. The *tiny, mad idea* was the beginning of the *doing*, believing it could separate from perfect Oneness. That is *doing* something. Then it does more by erecting a thought system of separation, sin, guilt and fear that then results in our projecting it all out and making a body that *does* something. Bodies *do* something. Do not *do* anything with *A Course in Miracles*. Let its love do *through* you, which means it has *nothing* to do with you.

That is what it means: "I will step back and let Him lead the way" Lesson 155. I will step back and let Him lead the way, which is exactly the same idea of this lesson: "Let me be still and listen to the truth." Then truth will act through me. It will speak through me. It will think through me. It will move through me. It will activate my body, because in the end, I am only a lifeless piece of wood. I am a puppet. So I want the Holy Spirit or Jesus to be my puppeteer, not the ego.

That is why over and over again Jesus says this is a very simple course. Just stop what you are doing. "I need do nothing" (T-18.VII.6:7). What that is a correction for is "I need to do something because there is a problem here that needs *doing*. I need do something with my body. I need to do the workbook lesson every day. I need to go to work and support myself and my family. I need to put food in my body, etcetera. I need to do something." It is always *doing*. Bodies *do*, because they come from the ego thought that was the original doer. Separation was the original doing.

Now this does not mean you do not do things in the world, but you do not want to be the agent of the doing. "*I* need do nothing." We define the problem and then we think we have to do something about it. You do not do *A Course in Miracles*. You stop doing and then let its love and let its truth come through you. This is a course in *undoing*. That word appears all the way through; whether it says the Atonement undoes, salvation undoes, the miracle undoes, forgiveness undoes. It is always undoing. A line I so frequently quote from the workbook, "Forgiveness is still, and quietly does nothing. It merely looks, and waits, and judges not" (W-pII.1.4:1,3).

If that is the principle under which I want to live my life, then I don't do anything. I undo. I look at the lies and I say, I am not going to believe them anymore. I do not look at the truth. I don't pretend to understand the truth. I do not seek after the truth. I seek after the lies, and I look at them kindly and gently with this Presence of love and kindness beside me, and then the lies disappear. Then the truth and the love in my right mind is now free to just extend itself, and it has nothing to do with me. That is why your only concern as a student of *A Course in Miracles* is undoing your belief that there is *A Course in Miracles* and that there is a "you" who is studying it.

It is so easy to see when you slip. If you care about what other people do and say with it, you are saying there is a book that they are ruining, that there are people out there doing bad things, and you know what is best. It is like one arrogant thought after another after another after another that cascade in a kind of mélange of lies and falsehoods. Do not listen to the voices of the dead. Do not try to understand why *A Course in Miracles* came now or what its purpose is and all that. That is a detour. That is a smokescreen. That is a distraction. That is a defense.

All you should care about is, "I want to learn my lesson that I am a mind and not a body, so that nothing that seems to be outside me will have any effect on me." It is so simple. Do not believe the lies. Any time you find yourself caring about *anything* outside of you, anyone or anything, you know that is a lie. You are listening to the wrong voice. But that does not mean you become cold and insensitive; just the opposite.

What the world calls love and caring is really murder. Many of you know that awful line in the manual, in the section on healing that says continued concern is really hate (M-7.4:4), not love. Continued concern is *hate*, not love, because you are making the ego thought system of separation real. You are making the body real. How could there be love if you make the body real? Don't you know what the body is? The body is the embodiment of the ego. Don't you know what the ego is? Hate, murder, stealing, raping, usurping, and the world that arose from that thought has never left its source. It is the same thing.

It looks like it is loving, looks like it is caring and concern in this world: helping people. Whom are you helping, for God's sake? Help yourself, and then if your body is guided by love to help other people, fine. What does that have to do with you? If you think that is holier work than somebody who is a hermit, you believe two and two is four. There is nothing holy in this world.

Again, that is what the early workbook lessons are saying. Everything here is meaningless. The only thing that is meaningful is learning that everything here is meaningless. Your sole responsibility is to accept the Atonement for yourself (T-2.V.5:1). It is restated later on in the text as your responsibility is "*to deny the denial of truth*" (T-12.II.1:5). That is really important because that explains what accepting the Atonement means. It is not accepting something that is positive. It is looking at the ego's denial of the truth (the truth being that separation is impossible) and saying, I do not believe this anymore.

Acceptance of the Atonement *equals* denying the denial of truth. It is denying the lies because the denial of truth is the lie. You deny the ego's denial of truth. Still later on in the text it says, you do not realize that to say "yes" means to say "not no" (T-21.VII.12:4). *Yes* means "yes" to God, "yes" to truth, "yes" to the unanswered question, which is the context of that passage. "Yes" is to look at the "no," the ego thought system of negation of truth and saying, "I don't want this anymore."

Another passage says, "Your task is not to seek for love, but merely to seek and find all of the barriers" you have placed between yourself and love (T-16.IV.6:1). These statements could not be more clear. Your task is not to seek for love. It is not to seek for truth. It is to seek and find the *lies*, the barriers to love, and then to look at them with that sweet, gentle smile of Jesus or the Holy Spirit as they dissolve. It is that sweet, gentle smile that remembers to laugh at the *tiny, mad idea* and then remembers to laugh at all the expressions of that *tiny, mad idea* in the world of time and space in which we think we exist.

It means you do not take anything in the world seriously, meaning you do not give it power to affect the love and peace of God in your mind. That is what it means. It does not mean you become cold, callous and insensitive; just the opposite. What the world calls "caring and sensitivity and love" is exactly the opposite. It is *specialness*. It makes differentiation real. It says "there is a hierarchy of illusions" (T-23.II.2:3). It says some people suffer more than others. Some forms of suffering are more noble than others. Some people are more noble than others. One puppet is better than another puppet, just because you paint a happy face on one and an angry face on another? You must realize everything in the world of bodies, of time and space, is meaningless; *everything*. That is what it means that you do not listen to the voices of the dead.

(W-pI.106.2:3) Be not deceived by voices of the dead, which tell you they have found the source of life and offer it to you for your belief.

Do not believe anything anybody tells you as long as they *think* they are telling you something; as long as they think they have some pearls of wisdom they are going to share with you and enlighten you. If they believe that, run like hell, because they are going to drag you deeper into hell. That does not mean people cannot be helpful to other people. But they could only be truly helpful when they do not believe in what they are saying, because they realize the "words are symbols of symbols...twice removed from reality" (M-21.1:9-10). It is the reality of love; it is the reality of realizing we are all the same. *That is* what the help is. It comes in words, it comes in concepts, it comes in behaviors that are helpful.

If the people helping you, identify with the form of the help, their help is going to be *very*, very limited. But if the people helping you know that the words they are using, just like the words in *A Course in Miracles*, are simply symbols of a love that unites us all, that is different. Because then they will have no investment in convincing you of what they are saying. They will have no investment in your accepting what they are saying. They are just letting love extend through them. They know that if you reject the love today, you will accept it tomorrow, or the next day, or the next year, or the next lifetime. They will have no investment in your accepting their holy, noble truths, because they know that whatever it is they said or did came from this love that is within. And if it is within them, it has to be within *everyone*.

It is only a matter of time as to when people will accept it, and that is not up to you. Your job is only, as the workbook says at the end, to give "welcome to the truth" (W-pII.14.3:7). And you give "welcome to the truth" by undoing all the obstacles to truth. You "*deny the denial of truth*" (T-12.II.1:5). That is the acceptance of the Atonement.

Special Relationships

Q: Yesterday you said that the nature of the ego is, "If you meet my needs, I will love you. If you stop meeting my needs, I will kill you."

K: I think I said that, yes.

Q: I don't want to have any type of relationship like that within me. So is forgiveness the key to ending that relationship?

K: Well, it is not ending the relationship. It is ending the *specialness* of the relationship. We are not talking about the form of the relationship. We are talking about the reason your ego has given to the relationship. I do not know if you are saying this or not, but let me just make the point. You do not want to use that as a way of avoiding relationships because relationships become the *means* of learning to undo our ego. So they become classrooms. This does not mean you have to seek them out necessarily, but it also means you do not want to avoid them, saying, "I don't want to be with a person because I know I am going to screw it up." Well, you have *already* screwed it up because the problem is not what you do with another person. The problem is what you have done in your own mind by choosing your ego. Relationships are a natural part of being in this world.

Bodies have relationships with other bodies, whether you are physically with a person or not. Everybody has had a relationship with a parent. A parent, parental figure, surrogate parents; *everybody* has had a relationship with parents. That is how our physical life begins. Even if your parents are dead and there is unforgiveness, you still have a relationship with them. It is not a question of what you do with the other person.

It is a question of what you do in your mind. It would be a mistake (and I am not saying you necessarily said that), to say, "I don't want to have one more special relationship so I am not going to have *any* relationships," which means that all your past mistakes and all the guilt over your past mistakes you are keeping within you. Because typically, the way we work out our egos and our guilt is through projection.

The special relationship can be said to be the home of guilt. But the special relationship also then becomes the classroom in which we let *go* of our guilt. You do not want to go into a relationship out of fear you are going to screw it up again. But you want to go into it and say, "Well, this is a classroom for me to really learn how my ego gets exorcised and gets expressed, but I now know I have a Teacher Who could help me let it go.

Body versus Mind

Let us go back then to the point I was making earlier about the body and mind. I keep coming back to it because it is so central. One of the things I frequently say is that you know you are making progress with this course when you recognize that the "you" that is continually being addressed, the "you" that Jesus is always addressing is not the "you" you think you are. The "you" he is addressing is your *decision-making mind.* That is where the problem always is. It is very difficult (since we obviously experience ourselves as bodies) not to think that we are being addressed as the person we think we are. Once that happens, then you invariably will interpret *everything* in this course as being about bodies.

Another line I frequently refer to is the line that says, "You cannot even think of God without a body, or in some form you think you recognize" (T-18.VIII.1:7). The reason you cannot think of God without a body is because we believe we are bodies, and "Projection makes perception" (T-13.V.3:5, T-21.in.1:1). I look within first. I join with my ego's belief in separation and its thought system of separation. When you project separation out, it gives rise to bodies. When you project the thought of separation out, which is in the mind, it gives rise to a world of separation. Therefore, once I identify it with my ego's thought system of separation and I think about God (meaning my body, my brain is thinking about God), I *must* conceive of God as a body, as some kind of person.

Once I project the thought out and I think of myself as a member of the species homo sapiens, then when I think about God, He must be a member of the species homo sapiens, too; different, but still a member of that same species. When you read the Bible, obviously "God" is a person. He is a man. He thinks like we do. He acts like we do. That is why, again, in this course, God is described as a person. The pronoun "He" is used, which means He has *gender*. As I frequently say, He has body parts. He has arms, He has hands, He has tear ducts, He has a mouth, He has a voice; on and on and on.

What is important about that line, which is why I quote it all the time, is that once you identify as a body, *everything* becomes part of a body. You think of the author of this course as being a *body* named Jesus, and you think of *A Course in Miracles* as a body, named a book. Obviously, most importantly, you will think of *yourself* as a body. Once you choose the ego as your teacher, you are compelled (because *projection makes perception*) to perceive everyone and everything as a body, meaning as a separated entity.

The Name of God is my inheritance.

Lesson 184 on page 345 is, "The Name of God is my inheritance." It says all this right at the beginning.

(W-pI.184.1:1) You live by symbols.

That is because *we are* a symbol. We are a symbol of separation. Jesus or any other enlightened person, non-ego presence, is a symbol of the Atonement. But we are symbols of separation, of the ego.

(W-pI.184.1) You live by symbols. You have made up names for everything you see. Each one becomes a separate entity, identified by its own name. By this you carve it out of unity. By this you designate its special attributes, and set it off from other things by emphasizing space surrounding it. This space you lay between all things to which you give a different name; all happenings in terms of place and time; all bodies which are greeted by a name.

(W-pI.184.2) This space you see as setting off all things from one another is the means by which the world's perception is achieved. You see something where nothing is, and see as well nothing where there is unity; a space between all things, between all things and you. Thus do you think that you have given life in separation. By this split you think you are established as a unity which functions with an independent will.

(W-pI.184.3) What are these names by which the world becomes a series of discrete events, of things ununified, of bodies kept apart and holding bits of mind as separate awarenesses? You gave these names to them, establishing perception as you wished to have perception be. The nameless things were given names, and thus reality was given them as well. For what is named is given meaning and will then be seen as meaningful; a cause of true effect, with consequence inherent in itself.

"Projection makes perception" (T-13.V.3:5; T-21.in.1:1). Our mind has a wish to make separation real, to make the meaningless meaningful. Then we project it out, and we perceive what we have projected because we projected it to perceive it. We project in order to perceive what we have projected. And what have we projected? A thought system of separation. And when we project it out, it gives rise to a world of separate things. It is a projection of a thought that says, "I am separate from God. There is a space between me and Him. There is a space in which I now exist." I project that out, I fragment that original space, and it gives rise to billions and billions and billions of spaces in between billions and billions of separate things, and I perceive it because of that wish.

(W-pI.184.3:2) You gave these names to them, establishing perception as you wished to have perception be.

This is all a wish. Perception is a *wish*. It is a wish to see the world the way I want it to be: separated, differentiated.

There is significance to the differentiations because there was a significance to the differentiation I originally forged between myself and my Creator, which, going back to what I said earlier, I then demanded God acknowledge. "Acknowledge that I am *different* from You. I am separate from You. Acknowledge me as a separated thing," which, of course, God cannot do because I am not separated. It goes on to say in that passage, and then you "made of Him an unloving father" (T-13.III.10:4).

We fired God and instead we erect our *own* god. Read the Bible. You get a wonderful portrait of the ego god that we made up. This is a god who acknowledges us. This is a god who creates everything, and then gives us, man, the summit of creation, the power to rule and name everything. When you read the first three chapters of Genesis, God gives man power over all living things ("dominion," it says in the earlier translations) over all living things. How do you have that power? You *name* them. When you give a name, it is power. This is an ancient, ancient symbol. When you name something you own it, and you have power over it.

Who gives a child its name in the world of illusion? The *parents* do, and from that time forth, they govern what that child will be called. Well, that is what this is talking about. We give names to everything and when we do, we think they are real. We have given them power. We have given them substance. We have given them reality. And why are we doing that? Why have we all done that as one Son? Because that establishes that I have power. I have power over God to establish myself and give myself my own name. I am no longer Christ. I am who I have made myself out to be, and it is all *nothing*.

The entire thing is *nothing*. It began with a thought of nothingness—the *tiny, mad idea* (T-27.VIII.6:2). Elsewhere in the Course, it is referred to as a "puff of madness" (T-20.III.8:4). That is what the ego is, a puff of madness. It is *nothing*, yet we called it something, which meant we gave it meaning. Then we project it out and we miscreate a meaningless world that we think is meaningful. It is meaningful because we gave it the meaning it has. That is what the early lessons of the workbook are all about. The room around me has meaning because I gave it meaning. But I am the one who gave it meaning, which means it is meaningless because *I am* meaningless. In fact, I do not even exist. I made up a meaningless world, and then I pronounced it as meaningful; the *thunder of the meaningless*.

What you want to do on a practical level is see how you give meaning to what is nothing. Anything that smacks of separation is meaningless and is nothingness. Later on in this lesson, it says, you have to use the symbols, but simply to proclaim their unreality. You proclaim the unreality of the symbols by not giving them significance, by not giving them power over you, by not allowing other people's egos to determine how you are, how you think, how you feel, how you behave.

It is your defenselessness, it is your gentleness, it is your kindness that is what demonstrates that there is another thought system, not only in my mind, but in *everyone's* mind. You exchange the thunder of the meaningless for the soft, quiet remembrance of the meaningful. What is very helpful is to just see all the meaning and power that you give to things that in the end are not even there. We give it the meaning. We give the world its meaning, both ontologically as well as personally. The only thing in the dream that has meaning is learning this is a dream. That is the only thing that is meaningful.

The Course says that forgiveness is a "happy fiction" (C-3.2:1). It is the final illusion. It is an illusion, it is a fiction, because it corrects and undoes what never happened, but it does not breed further illusions. It helps us recognize that everything here is an illusion. Every response I make that I believe is contingent upon something outside of me is an illusion, is a lie. The only reason I have whatever the reaction is I have, is because my mind chose it. I want to use everything in the world of symbols as a way of getting me back to the source of the symbols, which is my decision maker's choice for guilt. That is the problem, and that is a meaningful choice, because that is the real choice. It is that that I can now undo. It is meaningful because it is where the world comes from. Everything else here is a distraction from that simple truth.

Responding Kindly to Others

Q: I have these feelings to stop the perpetual illusion of the ego. And when someone asks you how you are doing, that the correct answer is, "I am not, because I am not here."

K: I hope you don't answer people that way.

Q: Well, that is what I am saying. I do not want to perpetuate the ego any longer, so.

K: You will not have any friends.

Q: I do not have any friends anyway.

K: Yes, which is a perfect way to perpetuate the ego.

Q: I am sorry?

K: That is a perfect way to perpetuate the ego.

Q: Is to not have any friends?

K: Yes. Yes.

Q: But isn't the truth that I *do not* have any friends?

K: No, oh, God, no, no, no. The truth is that you have *one* Friend, and because you have one Friend with a capital "F," *everybody* is your friend. Then you meet everybody where they are. If someone asks, "How you are doing?" you do not give a metaphysical smart-ass answer. Then they will not like you anymore, and I will be the only one in the universe who likes you. So that is not good.

Q: So to come from a place of—

K: Of kindness: is to answer people on the level that they are asking the question. I hope you do not go to a funeral and say, "Why is everybody so sad? Nobody died."

Q: It is tempting, but…

K: Well, remind me never to die in your presence. You got my point?

Q: Yeah.

Healing as the Release from Fear

K: Can I read you something?

Q: Yes, please.

K: You may feel this was written specifically for you, okay? But it was not. It was actually written for everybody. It is page 24.

(T-2.IV.5) The value of the Atonement does not lie in the manner in which it is expressed. In fact, if it is used truly [in other words, if you were truly being kind and loving, which is what would be reflective of the Atonement]**, it will inevitably be expressed in whatever way is most helpful to the receiver. This means that a miracle, to attain its full efficacy, must be expressed in a language that the recipient can understand without fear. This does not necessarily mean that this is the highest level of communication of which he is capable. It does mean, however, that it is the highest level of communication of which he is capable *now*. The whole aim of the miracle is to raise the level of communication, not to lower it by increasing fear.**

You would speak to people where they are. This course is a wonderful example of that, because this course is one lie after another after another. This course is written seemingly to suggest that we are here, that we are bodies, that my body has to forgive your body, and that I should ask Jesus or the Holy Spirit what to do. In fact, there is one really blasphemous line. I mean it is so bad that Jesus should be drawn and quartered. It says you should, "Ask God what I should do, and God will tell you what to do" (W-pI.71.9:3). Well, God does not even know you are *here*! Why is the Course written that way? Because we are all in a deep state of fear and we all believe that we are bodies living in a world, and the idea of not being a body would throw us into a panic.

The Dreamer of the Dream

In case you fell asleep when I read that, let me read you something else. Now I am going to read to you from page 584 in the text: Chapter 27, section VII, paragraph 13.

(T-27.VII.13:1-3) You are the dreamer of the world of dreams. No other cause it has, nor ever will. [Which is saying; everything here is an illusion, that everything here is a dream and we have made it all up. Then it says:] **Nothing more fearful than an idle dream...**

"Idle" in the sense that it does not do anything. When a car is idling, the engine is running but it does not go anywhere because the car is in neutral. The mind's engine is running with the ego, but it cannot go anywhere because there is nowhere to go because there is no one who is going. It is an idle dream.

(T-27.VII.13:3-5) Nothing more fearful than an idle dream [which is the dream of separation] **has terrified God's Son, and made him think that he has lost his innocence, denied his Father, and made war upon himself. So fearful is the dream, so seeming real, he could not waken to reality without the sweat of terror and a scream of mortal fear,**

unless a gentler dream preceded his awaking, and allowed his calmer mind to welcome, not to fear, the Voice that calls with love to waken him; a gentler dream, in which his suffering was healed and where his brother was his friend. God willed he waken gently and with joy, and gave him means to waken without fear.

What this is saying is you do not go from nightmares to reality. You do not go from the nightmare of living in this world as a body, as illusory as it is (it feels very real to us), and suddenly go "poof" and disappear into the heart of God. There is a line earlier in the text that says, do not be afraid "you will be abruptly lifted up and hurled into reality" (T-16.VI.8:1). When you go prancing around telling people they are not here, and they are not bodies and you are not going to answer their very simple question, what you are telling them is, "Come on, already, wake up!" Well, they are *terrified* of waking up, and *you are* terrified of waking up, otherwise you would hear *their* terror of waking up and you would respond accordingly.

So you walk this world as if it were real, in a gentle, kind, loving way. You do not tell people they are not here. You do not tell people at a funeral there is no death. You do not tell people at a wedding, "What are you getting married for? That is a special relationship." You do not tell people dying of cancer in a hospital bed, "Don't you know sickness is a defense against the truth?" *That* is not kind and it is not loving; in fact, it is *hateful*. You would only act hatefully to somebody else if you were gripped with fear yourself. It is not only that you want to be gentle towards others; you want to be gentle towards yourself. That is what this is saying. Do not be afraid "you will be abruptly lifted up and hurled into reality." You do not just go poof like that.

That is why this course is written on the level that it is at. I have been saying also for thirty-five years, this course is written on a very low level, a *very* low level. Any spiritual document that spends so much time talking about separation and fear and guilt and hate and murder and flesh ripped from bone *cannot* be very high. Now its teaching is incredibly high. It comes from the highest possible Source: perfect Love.

But it is written on a level that meets us on the lowest point that we could possibly be at, that we are *bodies*. The Course itself is a wonderful example of that gentler dream. That is why the language of the Course can be very confusing, because it says nothing happened; nothing is here, God does not know about you, you never left home. At the same time it says all that, it is very specific about we have to relate to each other as bodies, we have to forgive other people, God is a body Whom we are supposed to talk to, and on and on and on.

I have often given the following example, it is a major part of one part of my book on Helen, and it was a very impressive teaching example. Helen, who was incredibly wise, knew this course before it came, knew what it said without ever having to read it, even though she wrote it down, and knew exactly what the ego was like. She was actually a brilliant psychologist, as well as other things. Nonetheless, for a long time, her relationship with Jesus was predicated on her asking him for specific things and his doing it. Most people know the famous "Helen shopping" stories. In the early dictation, Jesus referred to it as the "higher shopping service" (*Absence from Felicity* page 231). I was with her, so I could attest to it personally. She would be told where to go to find something, and she would go there and find it; very specific.

Now if we followed your example, Jesus would say to Helen, "I am not going shopping with you. I am not going to reinforce your dream." The incredible thing watching this day in and day out was how nonjudgmental Helen experienced Jesus as being with her, as she kept asking for very specific things. "What street corner should I stand on to get a taxicab?" which is very helpful information to have in New York City, especially during rush hour when it is raining. And she would get taxicabs. I would be with her: "Don't stand here; we should stand over there." And we would stand over there and within seconds or a minute, a cab would come. *That is not Jesus*, but that was how she experienced it.

Well, that is very specific, and her experience of Jesus was *very* loving, very kind. He was very gentle and nonjudgmental, even though it was obvious to her and to him and to me, when I was with her, that this was all a defense. Especially when Helen would buy things that she knew would not fit, so we would have to go back the next week to return it. It was like an ongoing saga, shopping, shopping and more shopping. Until one day (I have told this story other times), we left the medical center. It was a lovely spring afternoon, and we left about two o'clock. I asked my proverbial question, "What stores would you want to go to today?" We had a list of different stores we would go to. And she said, "No, we are not going to any store. 'It' told me" (that was her euphemism for Jesus), "it told me I don't have to go shopping anymore." And from that point on, we never went shopping unless it was for something really essential.

When she was ready to let go of the defense, it was gone. But what allowed her to do that was not experiencing Jesus as judging her for making the body real and making the world real even though it was obvious to everyone. Again, Helen was very wise. Helen knew exactly what she was doing, that this was a defense. That is how you want to be with people.

Lesson 155 says at the beginning that when you are right-minded you look like everyone else, but you smile more frequently and your forehead is serene (W-pI.155.1:2-3). You look like everyone else, you talk like everyone else, you communicate like everyone else but there is a peace about you. There is no judgment, and you are calm, you are accepting, you are defenseless. That is what teaches; not the metaphysical truth. So if someone says, "How are you doing?" Say, "I am doing great, how are you doing?" That would be the loving response. Okay? I would like you to have a lot of friends. You are a nice guy.

Asking Jesus for Specific Help

Q: Helen, being as advanced as she was in her close relationship with God, and she had her "shopping service" and all of that. I think it is okay for us to want the same thing; to begin our relationship with Jesus, to ask him, "Help me pass my test or…" Sometimes in the Course it says do not bring God into the world. Know what I mean? The different levels create not only confusion but guilt, for asking Jesus to help us heal this body, heal that financial crisis or whatever. I mean I just want to hear it from you that it is okay for us—

K: It is okay, it is okay, but it is only okay if you…

Q: …as the beginning steps to start the relationship of trust.

K: It is all okay as a beginning step if you smile when you ask him. Just let me amplify this a little; why it is so important and why it is something that I really emphasize a lot. If you go through your whole life as a student of the Course, always asking Jesus for specific help, you will never grow up because you will believe that you cannot do this without his help, which means you are saying he is different from you. You are separating yourself from him. And you are always seeing yourself as a little boy or girl with Jesus being your older brother who is always there to help you and bail you out, and tell you how to pass an exam, and tell you what street corner to stand on to get a cab, and on and on and on.

There is nothing wrong with doing that at the *beginning* because you are at least developing a relationship with a beneficent Jesus, instead of the ambivalent Jesus that most people have grown up with. That is all well and good, but the idea is you want to grow up. Using the metaphor of the ladder as I did yesterday, we are all at the bottom of the ladder. The bottom of the ladder is when we think we are bodies where we have specific needs, and we think there is a Jesus or a Holy

Spirit who will answer our specific questions and meet our specific needs.

The beginning of *The Song of Prayer* addresses that and has a section called "The Ladder of Prayer" (S-1.II). The problem with always asking Jesus is that you are denying the power of your own mind to make a problem and to solve the problem, which is what it means that you always remain a little child. Because the truth of the matter is, there *is* no Jesus; there is no Holy Spirit, and there is no ego. These are simply our thoughts that are personified, which is a very helpful schema to have at the beginning of your spiritual journey.

But you want to get beyond that so you realize, as you make your way up the ladder that, "*I* am the Holy Spirit, *I* am the ego. It is *my* choice." What Helen was doing, which was obvious and we spent a lot of time talking about it, was that she was saying: "I do not have it within me to know what street corner to stand on or where I should go to shop, but I will ask Jesus." That denies the power of your mind to *choose*. You are letting Jesus do it for you. That is what is so important.

As you make your way up the ladder (again, the bottom of the ladder being that we are bodies here), you begin to loosen your hold on being a body, on being an ego, and you increase your identification with being a *mind*. I sometimes say, there is like a gold rung, and when you cross that rung you know absolutely (not just intellectually, but experientially) that you are a mind. It is at that point you realize, probably for the first time, that the "you" that Jesus is addressing in this course is your decision-making mind, not the person you think you are. There *is* no person that you think you are. At some point, you really get it experientially: "I am a mind. I am the dreamer of the dream. I am not the dream figure. I am the dreamer. I am a mind, and that mind has all power in it."

Early in the text, Jesus quotes the famous gospel statement that says "All power in Heaven and earth was given unto me." He changes it around that "all power" in Heaven and earth "is yours" (T-7.III.1:3), which means we have within our minds the power to choose earth, which is a symbol of the ego, or choose Heaven. That is the whole idea, that we grow up to become like Jesus, which is we have the power to make a hell and live in it, or to remember that it is hell and that we really want Heaven, and to choose the steps that will lead us to Heaven. You will never get there if you keep asking for specific help.

Q: Even if we ask Jesus, ultimately it is the process that is going to help us discover that experience, not necessarily a conscious *decision* to know I am mind. It is the result of an experience. I ask Jesus to help me with this or I ask the Holy Spirit, which is the same thing. I mean ultimately isn't the goal to know that I am one with him, no matter if *think* of him as separate? Isn't that what the process will reveal to me rather than me causing that? That would be the effect, isn't it, that I would get?

K: Yes, yes. To go back to what we talked about right at the beginning, the process is one of being kind because when you are kind, you are not projecting anymore, and you begin to realize that this person is not my enemy. And then it becomes, this person is not only not my enemy; this person is the *same* as I am on the level of the mind. As you do that, you are releasing your hold on guilt, and that is what helps you up the ladder. That is the process. That is why the Course is such an incredible pedagogical tool as well as a spiritual teaching. Because at the same time it is so metaphysically absolute: there is God and there is nothing else, and it is unequivocal about that, we are also given very specific guidelines how to live in this illusory world, that being under the principle of forgiveness or the miracle or, as I keep emphasizing, kindness. It is all different ways of saying the same thing.

And it is in the recognition we are not separate that judgments and attack are seen as not justified (*never* justified), because we are the same. That is what enables us to realize that, if we are the same it cannot be on the level of the body because bodies are different. Personalities are different. Everybody in this room is different from everyone else on all counts. So if we are the same, it has to be on the level of the mind.

We have the chart up here. This is the body at the bottom and this is the mind here. The dominant part on the chart is the mind, of course, wherein we are all the same. We all have an ego (a wrong mind), we all have a Holy Spirit (a right mind), and we have the most important thing, which is this blue circle, which is the decision-making part of the mind that chooses one thought or the other thought. Whatever thought we choose, we become.

It is recognizing that we are the same; that is the process. It is giving up of judgment. And as I become more identified with my mind, I become aware that my mind has the choice to either choose the ego and at that moment become the ego (because we become what we choose), or to choose the Holy Spirit and become the Holy Spirit. The problem in all this is the ego has convinced all of us right from the ontological beginning that this blue circle is the heart of sin. It was the Son's decision to be separate from his Creator; *that is* the problem: the decision-making mind chose the ego, which said the separation happened, instead of the Holy Spirit Who said the separation *never* happened. When we choose the ego, we *become* the ego; and the Holy Spirit, for all intents and purposes, disappears.

We become this thought system that now is the home of sin, guilt and fear. The ego says, "This is so horrific we have to flee from it." We then make up a world and a body and take the thoughts of the mind and project them all over the place outside of us. What made the world, what keeps the world going right at this moment (because there is no time and space), is the belief that if we ever return to this blue circle, we will sin again.

One question that is frequently asked by students is: "Okay, let's say I accept the Atonement for myself. What is to stop me from sinning again?" Which, of course, is a very logical question. But that is predicated on the premise that I sinned in the first place, which means I *still* believe I am a sinner. It means I cannot be trusted. I do not want to go anywhere *near* here (blue circle on chart). And because I do not want to go anywhere near here, I continue to identify as a body. *That is* the problem.

That is where the resistance to this course is most centrally located, in our fear of recognizing we are a mind and not a body. That is why everybody tries to compromise the essence of this course. That is why everybody wants to bring God and Jesus into the world. Because if they are involved in the world, if they are involved in my shopping needs, *I exist.* Not to mention what my needs are: they exist! The body is real. I have Jesus on my side and in my wildest hallucinations and delusions I have *God* on my side, all because I am afraid of returning to this blue circle. Because if I ever really return, my ego tells me I will be destroyed. I will remember my sin, and behind my sin is God's wrathful punishment.

That is very clearly articulated in the section called "The Fear to Look Within." In that section it says, the ego tells you do not look within, meaning, do not go back to your mind. There *is* no wrong or right mind; there is only a decision maker. Do not go back to your mind, because if you do, "your eyes will light on sin, and God will strike you blind" (T-21. IV.2:3). Which is a nice way of saying God will destroy you. So we do not go back; we continue to focus on the world, on our needs, on our pains, our pleasures, all of our specialness because that is what keeps us rooted in the world of bodies.

We write holy books that tell us God created the world and the body. The New Testament tells us God so loved the world that He made His Son as a body and sent him into a world of bodies. Why? To redeem us from *sin*. That is why *A Course in*

Miracles will never become as popular as the Bible. *Never.* The Bible says everything in the wrong mind on this chart is true. God Himself agrees! There is a tremendous fear of realizing that we are *not* bodies. In that same section, after it says God will strike you blind, it says, but that is not the ego's fear. The ego's fear is what if you looked within—went back to the blue circle—and saw there was no sin (T-21.IV.3:1). That is the *real* fear.

That is what is in back of an earlier section that says, "You are not afraid of crucifixion. Your real fear is of redemption" (T-13.III.1:10-11). That is the fear, because if I go back here and I look with Jesus beside me, I will realize everything in this wrong-minded box is not there, the whole thing was made up, there is no "I." That is the fear. All this would just fade away and I would be back in the Heaven I never left, except in dreams. *That is* the fear, and that is what continually drives us to be in the world, to be in the world of bodies.

The Decision Maker

Q: I don't understand if that little blue ball (on the chart) goes back to the blue circle. It looks from the diagram as if it still has not made the decision.

K: That is right. It cannot make a decision unless it knows it is a decision maker. That is why the word "decision maker" is there. And then there is a line in the Course that says who with the Love of God beside him would "find the choice of miracles or murder hard to make?" (T-23.IV.9:8) A line I quote often says that the miracle establishes you dream a dream (that is this blue circle), and its content is not true (T-28.II.7:1). Once you get back here and you look, you realize the whole thing is made up. The purpose of the Course is to get us back to this blue circle. That is what the miracle does. Once we are there, it is done. Okay? Does that help?

Q: Yeah. So once we are in that circle, there is no decision to make.

K: Well, there is a decision to make, but it is a no-brainer or a no-minder. Because once you are back here, and who with the Love of God beside him would find the choice between miracles and murder hard to make? (T-23.IV.9:8) Actually, once we are here, we are there for just a split instant (not even a *full* instant), a split instant, and then it is over, which is why we are hell-bent on not getting back there, because we cherish our individuality. We cherish our separated, special self. That is the problem.

The whole purpose of this course, the whole purpose of forgiveness and the miracle is to get us back to this blue circle (chart). That is it, and we fight like hell not to do that. That is why bringing God and Jesus into the world is so effective as a defense because now it has the mantle of spirituality around it. "Of course I am a body. God notices me. Jesus tells me where to go." As long as I keep seeing him as an older brother, I am seeing separation. I am seeing him as a person. I am a person, which means I am still at the bottom of the ladder as a body.

Q: The other thing was why do you say the Course will never be as popular as the Bible?

K: I am just being ornery. My hope is that the Course will have maybe sixteen, seventeen students, that is all. Hopefully in the end, only one student; I am just difficult sometimes. It is Monday. Monday is a bad day. Yes, I may be nicer tomorrow afternoon.

Dealing with Symptoms of Manic Depression

Q: There is a creation that my partner and I keep going, and it is just so painful. I really would like to stop creating it. He has a diagnosis for manic depression, and it seems to be so difficult to really live my own beautiful life and not have that affect me at all. Similarly, for him, he studies the Course two hours every morning and takes it into all his days, and still obviously we have a belief that manic depression exists. I would *love* to let that go. Can you say something about that?

K: Well, do you love him and care for him? Then what difference should it make what disease he has, whether it is physical or mental?

Q: It does not; it does not make any difference to the love.

K: So then there is no manic depression. Then his having manic depression would be no different from his having brown eyes or blonde hair or being six foot two, or whatever other characteristics of him. It would just be another part of who he is on the level of form. Your challenge, then, is to continually look beyond the form to this person whom you love and care about, and want to feel that he is the same as you. At the same time, he wants to learn that you are the same as he is. That is all, without denying what the symptoms are, and they can be quite disconcerting at times.

You should seek, as I am sure he does, anything that would help him on whatever level, whatever his belief system is. Regardless of that, you want to be there for him. And your lesson is not to let his symptoms disturb you or disrupt your peace and your love. And that goes for anyone in any relationship. Forgive yourself when it *does* disrupt you and say, "Well, obviously, it is disrupting me because I want it to." It is the same kind of thing I have been saying. Before I get upset by an episode he might have, I have chosen to be upset because I feel guilty that *I* pulled away from love, and I threw the peace of God away. Now I need something outside of me to put it on so I do not have to feel guilty.

If you are in your right mind all the time, which is the goal, then his mood-shifts would have no effect on you. It might have an effect on your behavior, but it would have no effect on your state of mind, and that is the lesson. When the Course says we should lift ourselves above the battleground

(T-23.IV), (which really means to be on the level of the mind—the dreamer and not the dream), then everything is different. That is where you want to go because that is where everyone wants to go. You want to be above the battleground. When what goes on, on the battleground of what we call "life" upsets you, it is because, again, you want it to.

But your goal is to be above the battleground as often as you can, until one day it is one hundred percent of the time. But what is *most* important is to forgive yourself when you do not do it, and to try to catch yourself as soon as possible when you are ignoring or denying the fact that you pushed love away, and now you are putting it on something external. Just be kind and patient with yourself as you are learning to be kind and patient with him. And that is immensely doable because even when you are in your ego state, you could be in a non-ego state by not judging yourself. In that sense, you cannot lose. But it *is* important that you see the relationship as part of *your* spiritual path that you chose, just as it would be for him and other important people in your life. Therefore, since you chose it, you want to learn from it.

Your fear would want you *not* to learn from it, but to suffer from it. But your right mind would see it as a wonderful opportunity of learning what love is, and love is not one body to another or one person to another. Love is a state of mind, and in that love, then, this person and you are the same. And so the symptoms cease to be front and center. They are now like the background, and what is front and center is your purpose. The Course talks a great deal about *purpose*, and it talks a great deal about *means and end*. When you choose the end or the goal, which would be to awaken from the dream, to be back as a dreamer and not a dream figure, you will see everything in your life as a means to attain that goal.

There are two parallel sections, one called "Setting the Goal" (T-17.VI), and the other called "The Consistency of Means and End" (T-20.VII), and they both virtually say the same thing. *You* set the goal, and if the goal is to reinforce the dream, then everything that you experience will be the means to attain that end. It will make you angry, upset, and special. If your goal is to be the *dreamer* and awaken from the dream, then everything—a current relationship or anything that happens day to day—would be seen as a means to remind you, "Ah, that is my goal."

An inherent part of that, and again, it is central, is to be aware that when you do not do it, it is not a sin. Do not judge yourself when you still become enamored of the dream. So again, you could be in an ego state and still turn it into a very powerful and helpful learning experience by not judging yourself. Because when you do not judge yourself for choosing your ego, you are going back to that original moment when we chose the *tiny, mad idea* and remembered not to laugh at it, and took it seriously (T-27.VIII.6:2).

Lesson 95 is a wonderful discussion of that. Lesson 95 talks about that very issue when you forget to do the workbook lesson (W-pI.95.9). Remember, the goal is to remember to laugh, which is the correction for having taken the *tiny, mad idea* seriously, and then all the shadowy fragments that have emanated from that *tiny, mad idea.* When you find yourself having chosen your ego, and getting angry or upset or guilty or whatever, realize, "Oh, I am taking the *tiny, mad idea* seriously." I could simply say, "Oh, I forgot what this was and I made the separation real, but I do not have to judge myself for it."

Q: In the middle of a depression, he will say, "I know all this is true but I cannot feel it." So the idea would be at that moment also to say, "I know that it is true. I cannot feel it and I forgive myself."

K: You mean for him?

Q: Yes.

K: Yes, and for *you* to say to him, "Darling, then I will feel it for you," or words to that effect.

Q: Thank you.

Example of Forgiveness Experience with Abusive Mother

Q: I just wanted to share a brief and hopeful story about the principle that there is no order of difficulty in miracles. My mother was very ill; later was diagnosed as schizophrenic. I am not going to go into the story of my childhood because I don't believe it, but it was very abusive physically, and I was terrified of her. As a little girl I was beaten within an inch of my life many times, and as an adult was just terrified of her. That is when she was diagnosed as mentally ill and drug-addicted to prescription drugs, and alcoholic, etcetera.

But in the middle of all this chaos I discovered the Course and had to go back to Chicago because she was going to be hospitalized again. One of the many blessings doing the exercises in the Course gave me was the last moment. I did not know at the time that this was the last time I was going to see my mother alive. But because I was so terrified of her, I could not see her innocence. That is what I was praying for because I had to go and see her. I was very afraid. I was praying just for the light of God to be in my mind when I interacted with her. I could tell on the phone (I don't know if she had been drinking), but she was in one of her moods.

When I went in, just as I feared, she started to attack me and, again, I was very terrified. I used to feel that she was going to kill me. That is how I was going to die. I was just terrified. I was deep into the illusion, and while telling myself this is an illusion, still terrified, shaking. While in the prayer that I was asking for light, I remembered my exercise for that day was, "I could see peace instead of this" (W-pI.34). As she started to get more violent in her behavior and coming into me, for the first time in my life I did nothing, and I just sat there and I thought, "I could see peace instead of this." Then I thought, "*How* can I see peace instead of this? Help me see peace instead of this." And I just thought, "You know, I just want to flood my mother with the love and light of God. I just want to be a channel for the love and light of God."

She was getting closer, and she was getting more agitated, and I just looked at her. And in the middle of all this she stopped. I guess I was crying and I did not realize it. She looked me in the eyes, and I don't remember my mother ever looking me in the eyes. And she said, with like caring and concern, "You are crying." I don't really remember her ever saying anything to me with caring and concern. Then she started to wipe away my tears, and we had a cup of tea. And I left, and she died shortly afterwards. But what I can say is that the Course allowed me to see the innocence in my mom, and if I could see it in her, I could see it in everyone. In the world of illusion she was mentally ill, and within that was a child of God.

K: That is a lovely story, Terri. I think it was earlier I quoted one of the lines that everyone has this spark of light in them. We talked about that. And regardless of what a person does, regardless of what happens or what illness is in a person's body (psychologically or physically), that spark of beauty is still there (T-17.III.6:7-11). It is obvious that what happened in that moment, which would be a wonderful example of the holy instant expressed in form, that when you made a decision to be peaceful, or even *wanting* to be peaceful (you don't even *have* to be peaceful; just wanting to be peaceful), that gave your mother a different message.

Your mother was waiting all of her life and all of her life with you for you to be defenseless, and when that happened she did not have to live anymore. If you (meaning everyone), could really see that, that is what really goes on in *all* of your relationships: especially the most difficult ones (parent/child, spouse, children, lovers, friends, close friends). People are just waiting for you to be able to be defenseless and say, "You have done nothing to me," even though they may have acted very badly, as your mother did. The world will use it as an excuse, "Well, she was mentally ill." But that is not why people act badly. And you have to look at this from another level, otherwise *nothing* here makes sense.

That "other level" is that blue circle above the battleground (on chart), and that is how you should approach everything. You get past the bodies, you get past the forms, you get past the situations externally, and you only hear (just as the Course says) the Holy Spirit's Judgment, which is either someone is expressing love or calling for love. You do not have to know whether someone is expressing love or calling for love because, as a loving person (the loving brother or sister in Christ), your response will be loving. It does not matter. Everybody is waiting for you to do that, and your mother waited her whole life with you. The more you got upset, the guiltier she felt and more abusive she got.

There is that very important line earlier in the Course in the text that says, "Frightened people can be vicious" (T-3.I.4:2). But what it *really* means is *only* frightened people can be vicious. Someone who is in a state of love cannot be vicious. There is only love or fear. When you are in a state of fear you will be vicious, and everyone who is vicious *is* in a state of fear. Sometimes the viciousness is masqueraded and is in a love-costume, but it is still the same.

I think that is what went on your whole life with your mother. When you lifted the relationship out of time and space, it was like this entity, this split-off part of you, as you are a split-off part of her, was when and where you were both waiting for that moment. And your mother really did it again: reenacted the same thing she had been doing all your life. How old are you, twenty-seven? For twenty-some odd years, she was waiting for you. When you gave the right-minded response it told her she was forgiven. Then she didn't have to be here anymore. Then she could lay her body down, and that is a wonderful example of the holy instant in form. The *holy instant* is not anything behavioral. It is really in the mind, but that is how it comes across. The lesson to be learned, just as you were saying at the end, Terri, is that you want to generalize this to *everybody*. But every relationship is like that.

In the teacher's manual, there is an early section that talks about the levels of teaching. The first level is a "chance encounter"; someone you may meet only once. One example says, "A small child bumps into you, and you do not judge the child." It says, "Salvation has come" (M-3.2:8). Then at the second level, are the intense relationships circumscribed by time. The third level are lifetime relationships. So parents and children would be an obvious one. Once you meet the person the relationship is lifetime. But it does not matter what the level of the relationship is because relationships do not exist in time.

Salvation comes in the holy instant when you do not judge someone for having pushed into you inadvertently or advertently, or deliberately. Whether it happens with an instant, a very momentary brief encounter or a lifetime encounter (like you and your mother), it is always the same. When you know you are a mind that is how you look at *everything*. As a body there are certain relationships that are important that you have to work on, and on and on and on.

As a mind, you realize whether it is just a person I am buying a cup of coffee from, or a person I have grown up with who has been abusive, it is exactly the same. *That is* the generalization, and it makes no sense if you are a body. It only makes sense when you are a mind, and it is a way of looking that changes everything. It gets you past the form to the content.

Everybody without exception wants to know that he or she is forgiven. That is the only right-minded reason for coming into this world. The wrong-minded reason, of course, is to reinforce the fact that we *cannot* be forgiven. The *right*-minded reason, and it is the purpose of *all* relationships from a right-minded point of view, is that we want to know we are forgiven. That is the message we are waiting to hear from somebody. And because our fear and guilt is so overwhelming we will continually ask for help, often in very abusive, vicious ways. And if you are looking for somebody to pin your guilt on, you will take it as an attack and you will feel unfairly treated, etcetera, etcetera.

When you are *right*-minded you are looking for something else. Instead of sending out messengers of guilt, you are sending out messengers of love. The way you "send out" a messenger of love is to be ready to *deliver* the message of love.

"When you are desirous to be blessed, I'll blessing beg of you."

The next newsletter article (Lighthouse, 2011 # 1) will be on that. The line from *Hamlet* is in a very dramatic scene with his mother. He is basically accusing his mother of being complicit in his father's murder. At one point in that scene he says to his mother, "And when you are desirous to be blessed, I'll blessing beg of you." When you need a blessing that is when I will ask you to bless me. You needed a blessing from your mother, and the way to get that blessing was to bless her. We bless each other with our defenselessness. It is not a word you say necessarily. It is when you do not take the attack personally and, just as you said, realizing, "I could see peace instead of this" (W-pI.34).

The second half of that lesson, even though it comes earlier, is Lesson 5. "I am never upset for the reason I think" (W-pI.5). You *must* say that first in order to say the second. I am *not* upset because of your abuse of me, even if it has a life-time history. I am upset because right at this moment I am looking for a scapegoat, someone to blame for *my* being upset. But that is not why I am upset. That sets into motion the next step, which is that I could see peace instead of this.

Because if I am upset for the reason I think, *I am a body*, and I am upset because of someone else's body. Whether it is a microorganism that is attacking my body, like bacteria, or it is another person, or an animal, or a piece of food, then I will think I am a body. "You have attacked me and I deserve to attack back." But, if I am never upset for the reason I think, it is because I am a mind, and I am upset because I chose the ego instead of the Holy Spirit. That is it!

Once I am here, in the mind, I am a decision maker who could see peace instead of this. You cannot get to here without taking the pathway of the miracle, which is this line (on the chart). The way I get here is I first get upset [the ego always speaks first (T-5.VI.3:5)], and then I say, "But this is *not* why I am upset. I am upset because I am a mind that has chosen the wrong teacher." That immediately puts me back in the mind, at which point now I could choose. I could see peace instead of this.

Something in you said, "Enough already; stop with the baby business. *Enough* already; I am tired of blaming her for why I am upset. Her acting out has nothing to do with me." And that allowed you then to be defenseless, and that was the cue your mother was waiting all your life for. *That is* what you have to realize. People are waiting *all* of their lives for you to say those words, "I forgive you," and it is not the *words*. You do not have to say anything verbally. It is to be defenseless in the face of attack or judgments or insensitivity or rejection or whatever, and people *wait* for that. When you realize that, then everything changes. Then the whole purpose of your waking up every morning changes because that is why you are waking up, to give that message.

And people will wait. They will wait for decades, if not eons, for you to say that. Just as the famous "Helen and Bill" story: "There must be another way" (*Absence from Felicity*, page 83). Helen waited all her life for Bill to ask that question so she could join with him. That is what triggered off all the internal experiences that led (a few months later) to the beginning of the Course.

Again, that makes no sense from the world's point of view, a world of time and space. It only makes sense when you are back in the world of the dreamer, of the mind, then everything is different. You will see everything through right-minded blinders, which means you do not see anything extraneous. You only see what is important, the road ahead. That is why you put blinders on a horse so the horse only sees what is ahead.

Well, Jesus is always trying to put blinders on us and say, "Everything outside of this range of vision is irrelevant! What is important is to see only an expression of love or a call for love. Just as Jesus says near the end of the clarification of terms: I want you to be my manifestation in the world (C-6. 5:1). I want you to be my messenger in the world. I want you to be my voice, my eyes, my hands, my feet through which I save the world, through which I save your mother. That is what he is saying. I want you to be my voice, I want you to be my words and my feet and my hands through which I can tell your mother, your parent, your spouse, your lover, your child, your employer, your president, prime minister that your sins are forgiven. People will wait for you, and they will wait, and they will wait. You have to hear their attacks and their viciousness and their abuse as they are saying, "Please show me I am wrong." That is what you have to hear.

A number of years ago I did a workshop called, "Healing: Hearing the Melody," and I talked a lot in that workshop on *listening*, listening to the other person. I used musical analogies in that workshop. You listen to the other person. You have to hear, just like I quoted the other day Isaac Stern's wonderful line, "The music is the silence between the notes." You have to hear the call for help between the notes, which may be very discordant, very dissident, harsh, abusive, but you have to hear.

The Selection of Patients

There is a passage in the *Psychotherapy* pamphlet; it is Chapter 3, section I, paragraph 2. This is talking about how the therapist selects his patients, but this has much, much wider implications.

(P-3.I.2:1-6) Who, then, decides what each brother needs? Surely not you, who do not yet recognize who he is who asks. [Now, he is not your patient; he is your brother, which means he is your savior.] **There is Something in him that will tell you** [who he is]**, if you listen. And that is the answer; listen. Do not demand, do not decide, do not sacrifice. Listen.**

It is all about *listening*. When you listen through the ears of Jesus you will hear everybody saying, "Please tell me I am forgiven." That is it! That is all anybody is asking. That is the only right-minded reason for anybody being here: "Please show me I was mistaken about choosing my ego. Please show me I am forgiven." The wrong-minded reason is, "Please show me I am right! I *am* an ego, and I want you to reinforce that thought system." But when you are right-minded, and you have that *little willingness* to be wrong (T-24.in.2:1), and therefore *happy* (T-29.VII.1:9), you will hear the most vicious attack as a plaintive call that says, "*Please*, please tell me I am forgiven, and I will continue to attack you until you do." And even if you genuinely forgive and they *still* attack you, you will not hear it as an attack.

Teaching and Healing

Just like Jesus tells us earlier in the text, you will hold that loving, kind thought until they could accept it, on the level of the mind. Let me just read you the passage where he says that. It is page 83 in the text, Chapter 5, section IV, paragraph 8.

(T-5.IV.8:1-4) How can you who are so holy suffer? All your past except its beauty is gone, and nothing is left but a blessing. I have saved all your kindnesses and every loving thought you ever had. I have purified them of the errors that hid their light, and kept them for you in their own perfect radiance. [And then he goes on.]

It is very, very beautiful. In a sense, it is like the first time in the text where Jesus is actually singing. You could feel it. Well, that is what you do. When somebody is abusing you and attacking you, and you are kind, Jesus takes your kindness and *holds* it for that person until he or she is ready to accept it. Since in that right-minded moment you and Jesus are the same, you are doing the same thing. It makes a nice story, like Terri's story, when the person actually can accept it, and there is a behavioral change. It does not always happen that way. In that case, it did; it is very, very lovely.

But whether it happens or not the holy instant was still there, and if your mother continued to abuse you, you were no longer holding it against her, which meant your forgiveness Jesus now holds in her mind (that is a *symbol*, but that is what he is talking about here), until the time she is ready to accept it. It may be this lifetime; it may be *another* lifetime, somewhere else in the hologram. It does not *matter* because on the level of the mind it is all the same. In that blue circle, that decision-making circle, everything has happened simultaneously because there is no linear time. *Everything*, all the sins, all the mistakes are there; all the corrections, all the healings, all the forgivenesses are there right in that blue circle: the *entire* world of time and space. That is where the loving thought is held.

But the idea is to be able to see that wonderful experience that Terri is talking about and see that in every relationship all the time *without exception*. And then forgive yourself when you see yourself making exceptions. When we are told in the Course that nothing happens by chance and there are no accidents (T-21.II.3:4), it does not mean that everything is divinely-ordained and Jesus is sending people into your life, or God has set this whole thing up.

They do not know about any of this. *We* set it all up. But relationships do not happen for the reason the world says. That is why I always say, "Do not believe two and two is four." Remember what we discussed yesterday in Lesson 106. Do not listen to the voices of the dead (W-pI.106.2:3). They lie. There is only one wrong-minded and one *right*-minded purpose for a relationship. The wrong-minded purpose is to reinforce the *tiny, mad idea* as being serious. The right-minded purpose is to remember not to take it seriously (T-27.VIII. 6:2-5).

Another reason it is so important to understand that God does not know about the *tiny, mad idea* (or anything that has seemed to have happened since then), is that He gives no response. If He gave a response, *something happened.* In the early parts of the text, Jesus says quite a few times we should take him as our "model for learning" (T-6.in.2:1), which, of course, is a wonderful idea. But behind him, you should take *God* as your model for learning. He did not give a response to the separation. When the Course says He did, that is a *metaphor*. That is a metaphor to correct the *ego's* interpretation of God's response to the separation, which we know very well. Just read the Bible! That is "God's" response to the separation, to sin.

The ego speaks first and is wrong (T-6.IV.1:2). The correction for that is God *did* give a response, but it was a kind and loving one. In reality, how could God give a response to what never happened? That is why He does not know about any of this. We should take *God* as our ultimate model for learning. So when Terri's mother started to attack her *again*, which it ended up for the last time, Terri did not respond, just as *God* did not respond. And the response Terri *did* give (which was her tears), enabled her mother to suddenly change. The tears (I am not saying that they were not sincere) were part of *your* larger plan of how to communicate to your mother your forgiveness in a way that *she* could understand.

All of a sudden she became a loving mother; maybe for the first time in her life! Instead of being a hateful mother, rejecting and cruel, she now became a loving mother and your tears set that up. That is how you have to see *everything*. It is not an understatement to say this course turns the world (literally) upside down so we look at everything differently; *everything*—one hundred and eighty degrees differently. Again, do not believe anybody who tells you two and two is four. Everybody in the world will *swear* that two and two is four! They will count on their fingers: "One, two, three, four; four fingers!" *What fingers?* Right? That, they *do not* say to you.

Two and two is *not* four. In the world of illusion it is four because there are laws. But that is not why things happen here, and that is not how healing occurs. I was talking about the *Psychotherapy* pamphlet, and it says it twice within half a page: healing occurs when the therapist forgets to judge his patient (P-3.II.6:1). That is not a two-plus-two-equals four world where healing occurs because the therapist does A, B, and C; has this intervention, he does this technique, he does this, that, all kinds of other things; all the things you study in school, which mean *nothing*. Healing occurs when you *do not judge*; when you go back to this decision-making part and you look at your patient and you say, "Nothing happened! You are not a schizophrenic. Maybe in the world of illusions you are, but two and two is not four."

A two-plus-two-equals-five therapist knows the only diagnosis is: *Son of God, separated type*. That is it! That is the only diagnosis. Anything else is a lie. You probably do not understand the real significance of that. When we were in school, everything now is different, but there were different kinds of schizophrenic states. I do not think they use these classifications anymore. So somebody would be said to have a schizophrenic reaction, catatonic type, hebephrenic type, simple type, paranoid type. That is where that comes from. But we are all suffering from the same mental disorder: *Son of God, separated type*. We believe we are separated. That is what you see.

Your judgment is, "Ah, this person is '*Son of God, separated type*' like everybody else!" It does not matter the forms in which that condition exists. Now from a clinical point of view in a two-plus-two-equals-four world it does make a difference. And I am not saying a therapist should ignore those differences. You do not want to go to a doctor with a ruptured appendix and he says, "Oh yes, sure, you are *Son of God, separated type*." I am not being stupid about this.

If you are a therapist, if you are a clinician of any kind in any field, you should know your field; just do not take it seriously. Realize the reason that patient is in your office is not for the reason he or she or *you* think. That person is in your office to be told, "Your sins are forgiven." I will act, for example, as a therapist in a way that will be kind and non-judgmental. Yet even though I may act in a very clinically-professional way, I do not believe it.

You will always act and treat the person with respect and with kindness and with gentleness, whether you are talking about a patient, whether you are talking about a lover, a child, a friend, a parent, colleague, it does not matter. It is always the same. That is why it is so important to understand the first law of chaos (T-23.II.2:3) and the first principle of miracles (T-1. I.1:1): there is no hierarchy of illusions. There is a *seeming* hierarchy of illusions. A slight neurosis is better to have than manic depression or psychosis. A splinter is better to have than a damaged heart. There is a hierarchy of illusions.

Well, in a two-plus-two-equals-four world that is true, and it is helpful to make such delineations, but that will not get anybody home. In the first principle of miracles, even though it happens twenty-three chapters *earlier* than the laws of chaos, it says "There is no order of difficulty [among] miracles" (T-1.I.1:1), because every problem is the same, every illusion is the same. That is the mindset this course attempts to inculcate in us, that we really understand that every problem is the same. Everybody is calling—out of the same need. They are calling out for the same message.

No matter what your business is, no matter what the forms of your relationships are, no matter what the forms of relationships are with your own body, we are asked always to be kind and respectful and gentle, and not to judge. When our situation calls for some objective judgment, we do not take the judgment seriously. If you are a teacher, you obviously have to make a judgment whether a pupil is giving a correct answer or *in*correct answer; otherwise you are falling down on the job. You are not being very helpful.

But you do not judge the student for being wrong or for being right. You do not love a student who is smart more than a student who is not smart. There is no hierarchy of illusions. There is no order of difficulty in miracles. *Every* problem is the same, every *solution* is the same. And that will enable you, again, to really listen and really hear what people are asking for.

"Beware of the temptation..."

But if you have a need to be unfairly treated, you will believe people are persecuting you and treating you unfairly. That is why there is that very important line, "Beware of the temptation to perceive yourself unfairly treated" (T-26.X.4:1). It is a very important line. Why is that line there? Because: we *all* are tempted to perceive ourselves unfairly treated. Why do you think we wrote our scripts with *parents*? We are not stupid! We wrote a script with parents who would treat us unfairly. Even the most loving parent in the world at times would treat us unfairly. The parent will have a bad day. It is purposive.

You cannot avoid as a child feeling unfairly treated. So Terri's case is one of hundreds and hundreds of thousands where children are abused; physically abused, emotionally abused. As a child you cannot avoid feeling unfairly treated, cannot avoid being afraid. You cannot avoid adopting certain defensive maneuvers to escape from the pain and the abuse. But we are not children anymore and, as adults and as *spiritual* adults, or as people *wanting* to become a spiritual adult, we now look back on that and say, "Yes, it is understandable that I would feel this way as a five-year old, but I am not a five-year old anymore. I can now realize that my disturbed mother, my abusive mother was really calling out for help and is simply waiting for me to tell her, her sins are forgiven. That changes *everything.*

Do not be deceived by appearances! Another line I quote all the time is, "Nothing so blinding as perception of form" (T-22.III.6:7). Nothing so blinding as perception of form; do not believe what your eyes tell you. And, above all, do not believe what *other* people tell you about what you are seeing. They do not know! They do not know about a mind. They do not know that the only right-minded reason people come into this world is to hear those healing words: "I forgive you. Nothing happened." The ego is the great principle of the *something happened.* The Holy Spirit is the great principle of the *nothing happened.*

You cannot say that as a little child who is being beaten up, sexually abused, physically abused, emotionally abused. You cannot say nothing happened. But as an adult looking back on it you could say, "Now I understand. Nothing happened." As an adult being abused right now I could say, "Nothing happened, because *I* have the power to see peace instead of this." That is the key idea. The "I" in that lesson ["I could see peace instead of this" (W-pI.34)] is not Terri; it is not Ken. It is the decision-making mind, that blue circle (on chart), otherwise you cannot forgive. You *cannot* forgive another body; you *cannot* forgive another person because you see them as a *person*! That is what the pamphlet calls *forgiveness-to-destroy* (S-2.II). You make the sin real and then you forgive it.

That does not work. You could only forgive as a mind forgiving another mind because you recognize, "My mind wants you to treat me unfairly. My mind wants me to suffer at your hands." "Behold me, brother, at your hand I die" (T-27. I.4:6). "Behold me, mother, at your hands I stand abused and scarred for life." Now again, that makes no sense if you are a body; bodies do hurt other people, other bodies. The Course says, "Are thoughts dangerous? To bodies, yes!" (T-21. VIII.1:1-2) Unkind thoughts lead to unkind actions that lead to suffering and hurt, but we are not a body. That is why it is so important to begin to see the importance of breaking that identification. You do that gradually, slowly, gently, kindly by seeing people as the same.

If I see you as the same as I am, then you *cannot* be a body because our bodies are not the same. Our personalities are not the same. Our experiences are not the same. We are only the same on the level of the mind. My wrong mind and your wrong mind want to be right: we are unfairly treated and, therefore, we deserve to attack back. Our *right* minds say, "I want to learn the lesson that I *cannot* be hurt." My body can be hurt, my bodily and psychological/physical feelings can be hurt, but I am not my body. I am not my feelings. My world does not collapse because you are unkind, and my world does not soar towards the heavens because you are kind. When I am right-minded, I realize it does not make any difference.

I want to be able to still my neediness; still my ego's voice enough that I could really hear your call for help. And, as your loving brother or sister, I want to return that call for help with love. I want to respond to that call for help with love, which means being defenseless.

Terri's wonderful example could serve as a model for how we should be all the time with *everyone*, with every *thing*. When your car does not start and you get angry at the car, you are blaming the car for your being upset. That is not true. You are upset because you *wanted* your car not to start, because that explains (and everybody would agree in a two-plus-two-equals-four world) why I am upset. My car would not start and I have an appointment so I will be late. You could only be late for an appointment in a world of time. Now I am not saying you should be cavalier about missing appointments, but be aware that is not why you are upset.

Again, this is a totally different way of looking at *everything*. Everything the world does and says (just to go back to the theme of the class) is the *thunder of the meaningless*. Being abused is the thunder of the meaningless. It screams out for justification: "Look how I have been unfairly treated." I have always said that is the hardest part of the Course to accept. I have said the hardest part of the Course to practice is that we are all the same. The hardest part of the Course to *accept* is the idea (being the line that comes near the end of the text), "...in your suffering of any kind you see your own concealed desire to kill" (T-31.V.15:10).

You *want* to be abused, you *want* to suffer because, again, that enables you to say, "Behold me, brother, at your hand I die" (T-27.I.4:6). In the preceding page of that statement, which comes from "The Picture of Crucifixion" at the beginning of Chapter 27, it says your brother's sins "are writ in Heaven...and go before him" (T-27.I.3:2). "I want your sins against me to be writ in Heaven where God will see them, and then God will punish you. And if He punishes you He cannot punish me because it is *one or the other*."

What is it that firmly establishes you are the sinner? My suffering: my pain. That is why that section is called "The Picture of Crucifixion." We are always walking around like poor Jesus on the cross, like this [Ken stretches out his arms], inviting people: "Drive another nail in! I want to spurt more blood. Do it, please!" Because then *your* sins will be writ in Heaven! And so I could say, "Behold me, brother, at your hand I die" (T-27.I.4:6), which means my body might die but God is going to lead me to eternal life, and you are going to go to hell.

That is why the world invented such strange concepts as *heaven* and *hell* and, if you are Catholic, there is *purgatory*—very, very strange. And, of course, even stranger is to believe that God sanctions that. We all go to Heaven or we all remain in hell; it is *one or the other*. It is "together, or not at all" (T-19.IV.D.12:8). We remain in hell or we go to Heaven. But we cannot go alone. We are not different. We are the same. If you are a sinner, *everyone* is a sinner including Jesus or any other enlightened person. If you are forgiven, *everyone* is forgiven, including Jesus. There can be no exclusions. Either we all go to hell or we all go to Heaven. There is only one Son, and what you do with one part of that Sonship you do with *all* the Sonship.

Again, what this calls for is a totally different way of looking at *all* your relationships. Do not see them as the world sees them. To go back to Teresa's example with her mother; if you look at it from the way we are talking about it, the way the Course talks about it, you see this as a wonderful opportunity. This is how you learn the meaning of love, because it transcends form.

You *cannot* love someone you perceive as a body; you *cannot*. That is why the Course says love without ambivalence is impossible in this world (T-4.III.4:6). *Everything* is ambivalent because you have a wrong and a right mind. You could only love as a mind. It will be expressed in a body. You do not love everyone in the same way, the same form. But the love is the same. It just takes different forms, but the forms are irrelevant.

Whether you love a partner who has a mental illness, or you love a little boy who accidentally runs into you, you have to see it as the same. Love in this world is *forgiveness*, which means love is the letting go of judgment. Love is letting go of the illusion that what this person is or what this person does, has an impact on me. That is a difficult lesson, but it is the only way of getting past the perception that we are a body. That takes a lot of practice and a lot of vigilance, but it will reorient your whole life and your whole way of thinking, and it will make everything meaningful to you.

Form and Content

Q: Just to go back to what you were talking about before, I am going blank.

K: Is it about Terri and her abusive mother?

Q: Yes, you talk about how someone has been waiting all their life to hear you basically say (not necessarily verbally), that "I forgive you." I had part of me that felt such a strong need to have you just affirm that you do not mean in form. I don't mean the words. You mean defenseless internally, but it could be like terminate a relationship, it could be yelling at the person, it could be seemingly harsh with a person?

K: Yes, as long as you yell with a little smile some place.

Q: By the world's terms, it could look like you were yelling back or leaving a relationship or storming off angry?

K: Yes.

Q: I guess it could be easy to deceive yourself and say, "Well, I am really at peace inside, but I just slammed the door on them." There is no reason to think it necessarily would look kind and gentle?

K: No, it is not the form, right.

Q: Or staying in a relationship or anything like that?

K: Not necessarily, no.

Q: Why is this so important? I think, on the other side, you could adopt a motive seemingly to be kind and gentle in form, as a way of deceiving yourself that you are being kind and gentle, when in fact you are not.

K: Oh, yes, *kindness-to-destroy* (S-2.II), absolutely. Yes, it is not the form. The message is given on the level of the mind. How the body expresses that; it just does it. That is not your concern. Your concern is only not to take it personally.

Q: It could be a defense, if you have to take on a mode where you are always a little bit weak or kind and gentle by the world's appearances, because you are so afraid of even having expressed it in a way that might look harsh?

K: Right, yes, yes.

What would you like people to leave here with?

Q: Ken, honestly, if you could choose the experience you would love for the people that come to these classes to leave with, or to go with, or to be with, what would that honestly be in words?

K: *Kindness*; kindness; that they would be kind.

Q: Thank you.

"Give [errors] over quickly to the Holy Spirit"

Q: We have been talking about staying in the place where we acknowledge that we made a mistake that we are here, right, and that we are this body? Staying there is painful, and I don't know what to do right after that. But then I found this little line here that says, quickly turn it over to the Holy Spirit (M-22.5:10). I know time does not exist, but what is "quickly," what is the dynamic there?

K: Usually it is about sixty-eight years; that is quick. What it means by turning it over quickly is why delay feeling better? As long as you choose the ego you are going to be anxious, guilty, depressed, fearful, angry; anything but peaceful. Why delay letting all that go? That is what that "quickly" is. The quickness with which you do it depends on your willingness to be healed and your willingness to learn that you are wrong about yourself and your perceptions, and ultimately your willingness to let all this go and awaken from the dream and be home.

Previously I read the line, "How much do you want salvation?" (T-17.II.8:1) That is another way: "How much do you want it?" If you really want it, you will [Ken snaps fingers] go like that. In the workbook it says, "Why wait for Heaven?" (W-pI.131.6:1; W-pl.188.1:1) If you truly want to awaken from the dream and return home [snaps fingers], you will do it like that. If you are more honest with yourself, you will say, "Well, I don't know if I am quite ready to let all this go yet." Then the "quickly" becomes sixty-eight years instead of sixty-eight seconds.

Q: But my struggle is because we go back and forth, right?

K: You go back and forth. I am going to talk about that in a moment. Yes, we go back and forth.

Q: We go back and forth, and so I know that I am probably going to say things that are not loving, or I am going to feel attacked in this situation that I am facing, and then I say no, I don't want to go there. I know that is wrong-minded. I do not want to go there, "Jesus, help me. Be with me." And then I keep on doing that all day? Is that what I do?

K: Yes, and part of that is understanding what it means to say, "Jesus, please help me," or quickly turn it over to the Holy Spirit. There is a lot of confusion about that, because typically people take sentences like that and they magically say, "Oh Jesus, this is awful. Please take it from me. I just chose my ego. Please take it from me." They *cannot* take it from you until you put it in their hands. "Putting it in their hands" means that you look at it, and you first recognize what you have done;

you recognize why you have done it, that you have expressed your fear of love again, and therefore, you have run into the arms of the ego. You have done that because you prefer the ego's gifts to God's gifts, and you prefer pain to joy. *Then* you have to be able to say, "This is too painful and this is too high a price to pay. I do not want to do this anymore." That is "turning it over."

Jesus tells us in the text that "together we have the lamp" that will shine the ego away. Then he goes on to describe how we have to look at the ego *with* him (T-11.V.1:1-4). Only then can we look *beyond* the ego. You first have to look at the ego and recognize, in the language of our class, it is the *thunder of the meaningless*. But then also recognize that *I am* part of that thunder. I am part of that meaninglessness because I think I exist; I think I am here. I think I am separated; I think I am special. As long as I cherish that self-concept I am not going to let it go.

"Turning it over" to the Holy Spirit or asking Jesus for help ends up being meaningless unless you recognize how much you *do not* want to let it go. I frequently quote the message that Helen and Bill had received one year into the Course's scribing. Jesus began the message by saying, "You have no idea of the intensity you have to get rid of each other." That is how the message began! (*Absence from Felicity,* page 297) And then it went on to say, "You have to really look at how much you hate each other." Then he explained, "Because otherwise, you will not get to the love that is underneath."

So asking for help really means looking at your decision for the ego and saying, "This was a horrid mistake that has brought me and probably others a lot of pain." Once again, whatever joy I thought I derived from making my specialness the central part of my life is not worth it anymore. It is too high a price to pay. *That is* what asking Jesus for help or the Holy Spirit for help really means.

Again, you cannot turn something over to Him without *handing* it to Him. And you are not going to hand it to the Holy

Spirit as long as you are holding *onto* it. You must look at what Freud, who was the first one who understood this and talked about it, called *resistance*. It is an *extremely* important concept, certainly in psychoanalysis. But it is extremely important for students of the Course to recognize how much you do not want to learn this course, because if you really wanted to learn it, you wouldn't have to learn it! You would be home!

The reason we need *A Course in Miracles* or any other spirituality is to convince us how much we *do not* want to return home. It is really looking at your resistance, looking at your fear to be without the ego, to be able to look at the fact that "I am *terrified* of losing *me*! Who would I be without my problems? Who would I be without my history, without my past abuse, without my anger, without my pleasures, without my pains, without who I think I am? Who would I be without that?" That is resistance. And that is the fear, because if you follow this course along and you take Jesus' hand on the journey, it will lead you home! That is why he says to us, "When you take my hand on the journey your ego will become retaliative" (T-8.V.5:6-7).

Self-Concept versus Self

Your ego becomes terrified. Many of you know this line. It comes right near the end of the text. It is Chapter 31, right at the end of section V, page 660, paragraph 17, sentence 6.

(T-31.V.17:6) There is no statement that the world is more afraid to hear than this:

When it says "the world," it means *us*, it means the ego. There is no statement that the *egos* in us are more afraid to hear than this:

(T-31.V.17:7) ***I do not know the thing I am, and therefore do not know what I am doing, where I am, or how to look upon the world or on myself.***

In other words, I do not know who I am. I *think* I know who I am. I *thought* I knew who I was: I was a child of my parents. I was born at a certain time, a certain socioeconomic status, etcetera, etcetera. I know all this but that is not who I am. That is who *this* is, a body in the world. But who I am in the dream is a *decision maker*. That is who I really am. And I will never remember who I really am as Christ, until I first know that I am a decision-making mind that chose *against* my identity in Heaven. That is the resistance. And then, of course, the final two sentences are what we are *most* terrified of:

(T-31.V.17:8-9) Yet in this learning [that I do not know anything about myself] **is salvation born. And What you are will tell you of Itself.**

That is the fear: I do not want to remember who I am. Because if I remember who I am as Christ, the "I" ceases to exist. *That is* resistance. While the word is not used all that frequently in the Course, it is used, but the concept is there all the time. Many of you are familiar with this passage, and I refer to it frequently. Right at the end of "The Obstacles to Peace" we have completed the long journey. We are right before the final obstacle, which is the fear of God, ready to pass beyond it, and everything will be gone and Jesus says: "Together we will disappear into the Presence beyond the veil, not to be… seen but known" (T-19.IV.D.19:1).

And there we are! After this long journey, we are right before the final veil, and what do we do? It says, "Your eyes look down, remembering your promise to your 'friends'" (T-19.IV.D.6:2). Who are the 'friends'? Sin, guilt, fear, and death. We get terrified! If I take one more step beyond that veil, I am gone! The "I" I thought I was, the "I" that I thought was a student of *A Course in Miracles* is gone. So, we become afraid, and we run right back into our ego's arms. That is *resistance*.

"Turning it over to the Holy Spirit" means looking at your resistance, because you would not have made it an obstacle if it did not serve the purpose of preventing you from awakening. That thought, that I need this obstacle to prevent me from awakening is *there,* so I have to change the purpose. I cannot change the purpose unless I know it is there. I cannot get back to Heaven and awaken from the dream until I first know that I *made* the dream. Nobody dragged me into this dream. Nobody dragged me into an abusive childhood, or anything else, or into a body that does not work right, or a body that is congenitally impaired and defective. *Nobody* did that. *This* (blue circle) did it; the decision-making mind did it, and it did it for a purpose.

If I want to get back home, the way back home is through the miracle, which takes us from our perceptions of the world and the perceptions of ourselves as bodies, and brings us back—not to Heaven. It brings us back to this blue circle (on the chart) where I am the dreamer of the dream. Only then can I look at my choice and say, "You know, this decision for the ego was a *bad mistake*. It was not a sin, but it was a bad mistake. *My mistake*, and because it was my mistake, I could do something about it." That is the good news.

At that point I choose my right mind, which corrects my wrong mind. Once I do that totally this wrong mind disappears; the right mind disappears because there is nothing left to correct. That is why the Holy Spirit is an illusion, there is nothing left to correct. There is no wrong mind, there is no right mind, there is no decision maker because there is nothing left to decide between. This whole thing disappears, and I am back where I never left, but there is no "me" there. That is the fear, and *that is* the resistance. More than anything else, that is what this course exposes. It exposes the fundamental lie that we want this course; the fundamental lie that we love God, that we love Jesus, that we love *A Course in Miracles*, and the fundamental lie that we want to awaken from the dream and return home. That is not true! If it were true none of us would be here!

The Course is a *correction,* which means there is something to correct, which is the ego. "Well, I do not want my ego corrected! If I wanted it corrected, it would be undone." That is what "The Unbelievable Belief" section talks about. There *is* no *ego* (T-7.VIII.5:1-2). What is the ego? The "ego" is the belief that the separation happened, but it *never happened.* Why is there an ego? And then why is there a world that arose from the ego? Because we want it so, that is why. Which means the only thing that keeps the ego and its world intact is our *desire* for it. When we speak about our desire for it, we are talking about this decision-making self that wants there to be an ego so that we could exist.

The most important part of this whole chart is this arrow right here on the chart, because this arrow is the link between the decision maker and the ego. It is this arrow (which represents what we decide or what we choose) that gives the ego its power. It has no power in and of itself. That is the *thunder of the meaningless*. How could what does not exist, what never happened, what *could* never happen have power? Hallucinations do not have power. But if you believe there are people out there to get you and that have power, it is not because there is anybody out there, but because you *believe* there are people out there. It is our *belief.*

It is the decision maker's belief in the ego, represented by this arrow; *that is* the problem. All of a sudden the meaningless and insignificant and nothingness becomes *thunderous*. Guilt is *thunderous*. It is a lot of action; it is a lot of noise. And then when this gets projected out it makes a very noisy world, but it is *nothing*. But we think it is something and, of course, we think that *we are* something.

The "Dynamics" of the Ego

"Turning it over to the Holy Spirit" is meaningless; it is just magic if you do not understand what the process is. It is looking at the ego. Just let me read you what I just quoted. It is from "The Dynamics of the Ego." It is Chapter 11, section V, page 202, paragraph 1. This is probably among the clearest statements you will find in the Course of what it means to ask Jesus for help. If people had read this and understood it, there would have been no *Song of Prayer* pamphlet, because that pamphlet was written one year after the Course was published to correct people's misunderstandings about what it meant to ask for help, and therefore, what it meant to forgive and what it meant to heal.

(T-11.V.1:1) No one can escape from illusions unless he looks at them, for not looking is the way they are protected.

"No one can escape from illusions unless he looks at them, for not looking (at the illusions) is the way they are protected." What am I saying when I say I do not want to look at my ego? I am saying it is too threatening, it is too powerful, it is too guilt-inducing. In other words, I am saying it is *real*. But if I do not look, its fundamental unreality is forever kept hidden from me.

(T-11.V.1:2) There is no need to shrink from illusions, for they cannot be dangerous.

Do not be afraid of looking at your thought system. Do not be afraid of looking at the world that arose from your thought system. Do not be afraid of looking at *anything* in the world. Do not be *guilty* about anything in the world. How could nothing be frightening? How could nothing be attractive or appealing? "There is no need to shrink from illusions, for they cannot be dangerous. We are ready to look more closely," because this is Chapter 11.

(T-11.V.1:3) We are ready to look more closely at the ego's thought system because together [this is what I cited earlier, "because together"] **we have the lamp that will dispel it, and since you realize you do not want it, you must be ready.**

There is a part of us that says, "I do not want this thought system anymore. That is why I am a student of the Course, That is why I am up to Chapter 11 and I did not stop with Chapter 1." One might think this is an assumption Jesus is making, but the fact is we are committed to this. But now you have to recognize what you are committed to. *This* is what it means to ask Jesus or the Holy Spirit for help. This is what it means to turn the ego over. It means looking closely at the ego's thought system; looking *closely*. Not just a cursory look; really understanding what this whole insanity is, this whole insanity of the wrong-minded box that gives rise to the insanity of living in this world as a body.

You have to look *closely* at this, and you cannot do this without joining with *him*. Jesus cannot do it without our joining with him. He says earlier remember, "I need you as much as you need me" (T-8.V.6:10). Obviously there is a different level of need. He *needs* us because otherwise he cannot help us. He also says earlier, "I will come in response to a single unequivocal call" (T-4.III.7:10). "If you really want my love and my help it is there, but it must be unequivocal. You must mean it. I will come in response to a single unequivocal call."

You may take it back a moment later, but there has to be a single unequivocal call that means, "I am tired of my ego. There *must* be another way." The help he gives is to hold the lamp that we now hold with our joint hands and we look at the ego, look at our *craziness*, look at the insane belief that somehow getting angry makes us feel good or getting sick atones for our sin against God, and all the other crazy things that we do; that special love is worth more to us than *true* Love.

It is really understanding how absolutely insane we have been. It is no accident that clinical terms are used in this course: *insanity, madness, hallucination, delusion*, and *fantasies*. They are used more than once. What is described in this book about the ego is a description of a *paranoid schizophrenic, literally*; except we are not talking about those people whom we lock up in a mental hospital. We are *all* paranoid schizophrenics. We all think the world is out to get us. We think germs are out to get us. We think the government is out to get us. We think *people* are out to get us. We think old age is out to get us.

We are psychotic because we think there is a world out here. The only medication that this course prescribes is *forgiveness* and kindness and giving up of judgment. "Let us be very calm in doing this," in other words, do not make a big deal about it. Do not be anxious about it, do not be frenetic about it, do not be frantic, do not obsess about it.

(T-11.V.1:4) Let us be very calm in doing this, for we are merely looking honestly for truth.

How do you find truth? By looking at the *illusion*. When you look at the illusion and you understand there *is* no illusion, there is only your *need* to have an illusion be there and that need is changing, the illusion disappears, *then* you find the truth.

(T-11.V.1:5) The "dynamics" of the ego will be our lesson for a while, for we must look first at this to see beyond it, since you have made it real.

That is Jesus' explanation for why this lofty spiritual teaching spends *so* much time talking about the illusion. People will say, "All I have to do is just snap my fingers—it is all an illusion and I am back in Heaven." Well, guess again. That is *level confusion* (T-2.IV.2:2). That will not happen because you are not aware there is that unconscious resistance. Despite what my intellect tells me is true, this unconscious resistance is there that says: "I don't want *it* to be true, and therefore, I do not want to get my hands dirty and look at the ego; after all, it is an illusion." It is like people who say, "I don't want to look at the news because I do not want to pollute my holy mind," and I bet you are one of them, right?

Student: Yes.

How did I know that? See, I am channeling again. [Laughter] The news cannot pollute your holy mind because it is already polluted. If you think there is pollution *out there* you are polluted! I am sorry; there is just *silliness* out there. There is a projection of a *tiny, mad idea* that never happened. The news is interesting because you can see, "Boy, I never thought of the ego that way." That is really ingeniousness. Each day there are more and more ingenious ways of expressing hate and murder and destruction and specialness. It is wonderful! It is funnier than a Woody Allen movie, all these expressions of the ego.

There is *nothing* out there that can pollute your holy mind. There is no one out there who could drag you into the bowels of hell. If you think there *is,* then it is because you are already in the bowels of hell. Then you project it out and you say, "The hell is not in me. It is in the news, it is in the world. It is in this person or that person." It is *making the error real.* Later on Jesus says (speaking of the original error, but it works just as well for all the fragments of the original error), do not call it sin, do not invest it with guilt, and above all, do not be "*afraid of it*" (T-18.I.6:7-9). Do not make a big deal about it, do not call it sinful, do not feel guilty, and above all, do not be afraid. How could you be afraid of what is not there?

What do you do as a parent when your little child wakes up from having a terrible nightmare? You comfort the child and you say, "It was only a bad dream, sweetheart. There *aren't* any monsters out there. There is nobody in the closet. What you heard outside trying to break the window was the wind rustling through the trees. There is nothing out there. Don't be afraid." That is what you would say. Well, that is what Jesus tells us: "Don't be afraid. Whatever is out there you *put* there. And you put it there because you want to see it *out there* rather than recognize it is in you." That is what he is saying here.

(T-11.V.1:5-6)...we must look first at this to see beyond it, since you have made it real. We will undo this error quietly together [in fact, he talks about looking at it with calmness, looking at it *quietly*; "quietly together"]**, and then look beyond it to truth.**

At that point you are not looking beyond the ego because the ego has disappeared. It is like you have truth here where I am standing, and then there are all the veils of specialness, all the veils of the ego. Once you look at them and you smile sweetly and say, "This is nothing," it dissolves and then truth is there. That is why this is not called "A Course in Truth," or "A Course in Love," or "A Course in God." It is called *A Course in Miracles* because the miracle is the correction. It is the way out of hell that takes us *from* hell (the world) back to where the hell originated. It does not take us to Heaven. It takes us back to this decision-making mind; *then* we can make a reasonable choice.

"Turning it over," means looking at how much I *do not* want to turn it over. What Jesus told Helen and Bill after the first year of the scribing, is before you could recognize this strong love that is there between you, you must first realize how much you hate each other (*Absence from Felicity*, page 297). The whole Course in microcosmic form is in that simple message, less than one page. The way you get to the love is to look at the hate. *Look at it.* The way you get to Heaven is to look at the hell that you made as a substitute.

Is there an idea of "Ken" within the blue circle?

Q: Within the Atonement or within the blue circle (on the chart), is there an idea of "Ken"?

K: Yes, in one sense, yes, because the entire world is in there. But the idea of "Ken" does not appear until this blue circle chooses the ego that then projects out and fragments into billions and billions of pieces. One piece is called "Ken," another piece is called "David," etcetera. This David too, except he is not here, right?

Q: So we were only ideas when we tried to leave our Source?

K: Right, but everything is in this blue circle in that sense, because "ideas leave not their source" (T-26.VII.4:7). The world out here is still in the mind of the dreamer. Dreams leave not the dreamer. The idea of "Ken" does not begin until the decision maker, once again, chooses the ego. This whole thought system gets projected out as one Son, fragments into billions and billions of pieces, and each piece has a name.

Q: Ken does not even live over on the right side (on chart)?

K: No, there is no name.

Q: No Ken there; not even an idea of Ken?

K: No.

The Ugliness of the Illusion

Q: I said it this morning: as the Son of God I *did* forget to laugh, and I do not know how to laugh at this. The illusion of my being, this is not funny. To see women treated the way that they are so horribly in the world is not funny to me. For the country that I live in, for people to spend money on luxuries when my brother on another continent has nothing to eat, but it is okay? In this illusion, in this life we are allowed to let you starve and me to be rich? These are not kind illusions. Is there such a falsity in my mind, that I am incapable of projecting a heavenly illusion? I don't quite understand the disconnect.

K: Okay, I think that is a very accurate portrayal of what everyone feels on some level. It *is* a horrible world, and when the Course says that we should laugh, it does not mean that you laugh at people's suffering and misery (W-pI.187.6:4). It means you laugh at the *source* of it, which is the original thought of the ego. Once that original thought is taken seriously, then the world becomes very serious and very destructive, just as you described.

The challenge, which is what makes this course *so* difficult in terms of practicing it—it is relatively easy to learn what it says after a while, but to practice it is *very*, very difficult. It is very difficult, because it is hard to imagine there is a part of us that is enamored of all that pain and all that abuse and all that filth and all that cruelty. We know we are enamored of it because we *see* it. And making believe we do not see it does not help, because you know it is out there anyway. Once you give the dream reality it is god-awful, and then you cannot laugh at it. Anyone who laughs at the dream believing it is there and god-awful is just a sadist. That is not a spiritual stage.

What you need to be able to do, what everyone needs to be able to do is to take those perceptions of what is out there and realize that these are projections. They are projections of an illusion, to be sure, but it is an illusion that in our distorted mind we still cling to. What you are describing, which is what I think almost *everybody* would describe, is our abhorrence of what goes on in the world, and the pain and suffering and the injustices and inequities that abound here.

What we really find so repulsive is the ego thought itself, which is that "I could make a world the opposite of Heaven. I could make a love that is better than God's Love. There is something other than the Everything that I want." And then the terror that I will be found out and I will be punished for it. That is everything that is encapsulated in this wrong-minded box. When I talk about sin, guilt, and fear, they are just words, but the thought and feelings behind them are enormous. They have a magnitude and a vastness that is beyond comprehension. Yet it ends up as nothing because all of that is a lie. Because the basic truth is we never left; that is the Atonement.

But the problem is, as I have been saying, to accept that and to get to that place you have to really say, "This self is not what I thought." That is very difficult because basically (just using you as an example, but it is everyone's experience) the "you" that finds the world abhorrent and finds the world repulsive is still a "you." There is still a "you" that says, "I do not want to live in a world where there is such hatred and cruelty and injustice." At that point it will never end. The nightmare will never end. No matter how you may try to screen it off (and everybody tries to screen off the horror of the world in different ways), it will never work. It will only work (and this is what takes time because of our resistance and our fear), when you recognize that the whole thing is based on a lie. All the ugliness and pain that we see in the world is a *projection* of a reaction to the *tiny, mad idea* that never happened.

The problem is this has to become more than just an intellectual understanding. It has to become part of your experience. You will know that you have done it when you could walk this world and *not* be affected by what happens here. Not because you are denying it or you are turning your back on it, or insensitive to it, but because you understand where it is coming from. That will help you realize that the people who are being victimized and abused are the same as the people who are abusing them and victimizing them, because nobody could ever hurt anyone else.

Nobody could ever treat anyone else unfairly if they really knew they were children of the Love of God. It is *impossible* to feel the love of that right mind and ever say anything hurtful, ever *think* anything hurtful. Anyone who is hurtful on any level cannot believe that they are children of that Love. The Course says, that one of the aims of specialness is to throw your brother over the precipice (T-24.V.4:2). It talks about flesh ripped from bone (T-19.IV.A.13:2); that is what torture is.

But it comes from fear. "Frightened people can be vicious" (T-3.I.4:2). You want to be able to look at the fear, not only in the abused, but in the abusers. When you can begin to do that then you know you are on your way home, because then you are beginning to realize that we are *all* the same. We are all stuck in the same miserable boat. People who inflict pain are in as much pain as the pain they are inflicting on other people, physically and/or psychologically. Now that is a big step. That is hard to do.

The Form that Right-Minded Love Takes

Q: As a lucid dreamer, do you have any responsibility? If I say something like, "I do not want to have the capability as a dreamer to dream of pain like this."

K: Right, but the way you could break that awful, vicious, murderous cycle is to, as the Course says, accept the Atonement for yourself. When you really identify with the Love that created you, that love would extend and embrace all people. You would look out at the world, you would watch the news, you would hear about something and your heart would go out, not only for the woman who is raped, but for the rapist; not only for the victims of famine and disease, not only the victims of bombs raining down on their villages, but the people who build the bombs, the multinational corporations that set up a world in which there are people starving, people who do not receive the medications that they need. Your heart will go out to them as much as to the people who are perceived as the victims.

That is the step you have to be able to take. And when you *do not* take it and you start being upset with people, then realize there is a part of me that I do not want healed yet. The only way I could have that part healed is to recognize we are all the same; but *all* the same, not just the "good" people. That is what it says.

Q: May I forgive the idea of this dream?

K: Yes, absolutely. But you will know you have truly forgiven the idea of the dream when the dream no longer affects you, okay?

Q: In the world of illusion, is there a difference between love and hate?

K: Nope.

Q: Is it fueled by fear?

K: Yep. [Laughter] I have one more "yep" left. [Laughter]

Q: What form does love in the right mind take?

K: It is kindness to all people, all things, at all times. That is the form love in the right mind takes. It is universal kindness with *no* exception. It is gentleness, it is patience for all people, all the time, for all things, all the time, for all circumstances, all events without exception.

Q: Is that bringing in judgment? Does that come in?

K: There is no judgment.

Q: No judgment?

K: Kindness and judgment are mutually exclusive states.

Q: How do you deal with the strong impulse to judge? How do you deal with judgment?

K: You do not take it seriously.

A Course in Miracles as a Lofty Spiritual Teaching

Q: But is there a way to catch it, before that?

K: What most people's experiences are after you work with the Course for a while, is that you become more and more clear when your ego's activated. The idea is to try and catch it as quickly as you can, and there are certain signs. The obvious ones: you get angry, you get anxious, you get upset, you get depressed. More subtle, but actually the cause of those negative feelings, is when you have a perception that doesn't make people the same; when you see people as different, and the differences you make to be significant. You keep looking for the signs. You begin to see that the only purpose of your waking up in the morning is to learn this lesson.

You do not wake up in the morning to do whatever you have to do, and we all have things we have to do every day. I am not saying not to do them. But you want to do them within the overriding context of, "I want to learn more about my ego and how to let it go, and how quickly I choose it." *That is the goal*. The things in form, the behavioral things I have to do would automatically flow easily and naturally from my right mind if I am right-minded. It is not that you do not do the things you have to do and fulfill your roles and functions each day. But you try and do it differently. That is your purpose.

It is a question of really being single-minded. "Do I really want salvation? Do I really want to awaken from the dream? Do I really want to learn this course? And if I do, why do I dillydally? Why do I keep taking detours?" And not to say that with an air of judgment about you, but to really see, "Yes, I am really afraid. I am ambivalent. I am not interested in giving Jesus that single, unequivocal call. I am *very* equivocal. I am very ambivalent. I am not sure I want to do this." That is very honest.

Ideally, if this is what you want more than anything, *every* second of every day would be spent on doing something that would take you closer and closer to the Atonement, and further and further away from your ego. *Everything* would be seen that way. Everything would be seen as an opportunity. When the text says every encounter is a holy encounter (T-8. III.4:1; T-13.IV.6:9), it is because it is offering you the opportunity of choosing holiness instead of guilt. That is what you want to think about *all* the time, no matter what you are doing; whom you are with. When that is not uppermost in your mind, then that is what you forgive in yourself.

In a sense, one of the purposes of the workbook is to expose how *un*willing we are to learn this course; just another word for *resistance*. Everybody, I think, who has done the workbook experiences forgetting. "Oh my god, I have to think of this every hour or five times an hour. I mean, give a guy a break!" Well, why am I not jumping for joy? I mean, this is my way home.

What could be more important than undoing my guilt and really becoming an expression of love in this world? What could be more important than that? What could be more important than waking up from this dream? But see how we approach the workbook or approach the Course or approach all of our daily experiences, and you do exactly the opposite! That is helpful. It gives you very helpful information as to the degree of your resistance. You want to become increasingly aware of that.

Q: A lot of times I wake up in the morning and I'll go, "Oh no." I can tell I woke up in my ego.

K: Right, instead of being joyful, "This is another day in class." Unfortunately, our education system has gotten so, so screwed up. Education should be a joyful experience; not one with anxiety and judgment and this and that. "I will have to do homework, and why do I have to do this?" It should be a real joy to learn. That would be the prototype of what, as adults, we would be grateful for learning. It is not an accident that the Course came in a curricular format: text, workbook for students, manual for teachers. It talks about lessons, teachers, all the way through. The Holy Spirit is our Teacher. Everything is a lesson, and that is not accidental. That is because this is a school.

Q: I have a feeling like I am getting erased and then I get fearful. Would that be another form of what we are talking about?

K: Yes, yes, absolutely. Before you become "erased" as "you," you become erased as "the you" who is angry, guilty, depressed, anxious, special, etcetera, etcetera. That is why it is important not to skip steps.

Q: Because a lot of things just do not have the meaning they had.

K: Right, but you know, nobody will take your ego away from you. You will let it go gradually as you are comfortable in doing it. The attitude we "*should*" have is to be grateful. I am in class and I am going to learn. I am going to learn the only thing that is meaningful for me to learn: "That all of this is a lie, and the truth is within me." But we do not greet that with joy. We do not greet each day with joy. We do not greet each workbook lesson with joy because we are terrified of what it means. You want to go slowly and work with that. That is my segue into what I want to talk about and that is the whole idea of this is a process.

The Process

As I said right at the beginning, the problem with the world and the ego being "the thunder of the meaningless," is that we are part of that thunder and we are part of that meaninglessness (W-pI.106.2:1). We are asked to study a course that will lead us away from who we *think* we are, and that is where the resistance comes from. That is why it is so important to understand this course really represents a process.

In a sense, that is what is missing (but I don't mean that in a negative way at all), in some other very high spiritual teachings, such as you find in the Vedanta or Upanishads. The highest teachings that you find in the East: there is no room for *process*. Many people have observed, as I have too, that Krishnamurti, who was a wonderful teacher, that metaphysically he and the Course are really in the same place. But there is no process in Krishnamurti's work. You are there or you are not there.

The Course is unique, I think, because it offers us this process. That is why I have always said, it blends together these very high metaphysical teachings with a very profound and sophisticated psychology. As I have also observed for thirty-five years, you would not have had that without the work of Freud. I always like to put a plug in for him. It is that integration of this very sophisticated psychology that describes how we function day to day, with this very lofty, profound metaphysical view that there is God and there is nothing else.

The Course really represents what I refer to as an *absolute non-duality*; a non-dual thought system where there is no way of fudging the fact that everything here is an illusion. But at the same time, we are guided very slowly, gently, kindly, softly how to negotiate and navigate our way through the dualistic waters of being here in a body; so that we end up back home. But it is really important to recognize this is a *process*.

Let me read to you part of a lesson. I read this every once in a while. It is such a succinct and a nice summary of the idea of *process*. It is in the workbook, Lesson 284, page 439. The title of the lesson is, "I can elect to change all thoughts that hurt." But that is not the issue in terms of what I want to read. Let me just read you from the beginning of the lesson.

(W-pII.284.1:1-3) Loss is not loss when properly perceived. [Because how can the Son of God lose?] **Pain is impossible. There is no grief with any cause at all. And suffering of any kind is nothing but a dream.**

Now what I am going to read to you is the idea of a depiction of the *process* of coming to grips with that truth. In other words, that everything here is an illusion. That is what this is saying. Everything here is an illusion. Everything here is a dream.

(W-pII.284.1:5-6) This is the truth [what I just read to you]**, at first to be but said and then repeated many times; and next to be accepted as but partly true, with many reservations. Then to be considered seriously more and more, and finally accepted as the truth.**

Again, that is a very succinct statement of *process*. You first look at this and get this intellectual idea, and you realize, this is the truth. At first you just mouth the words and you repeat them many times. Then you accept part of it is true, whatever part you want to say is a dream and say everything else is real. But you still have reservations. "I still like being me," as an example. Then you consider this more and more: "Well, maybe this is true and maybe this is true for *everything*." And then finally, you accept it as the truth, not as an intellectual formulation; you accept it as an experiential truth. You *really* know everything here is a dream, and *you are* the dreamer. You are a *mind*. That is what it means to be "above the battleground" with Jesus (T-23.IV.9:5). But it is a process.

I have mentioned other times *The Song of Prayer* talks about the "ladder." There is that section called "The Ladder of Prayer" (S-1.II). The top of the ladder is the real world. That is when you accept the Atonement for yourself. That is when your right mind has totally undone the wrong mind, which cancels out the right mind. There is no decision maker. That is the real world, and you are there but an instant. It says in one passage, "You will barely have time to thank God" (T-17. II.4:4), and then you are gone. Then God reaches down and lifts you unto Himself, a metaphoric way of saying everything disappears (W-pI.168.3:2).

The top of the ladder (the "ladder" representing our spiritual journey) is the real world, and God is beyond the ladder entirely. The bottom of the ladder is our experience here as bodies, as personalities, as individuals. That is where the Course comes to us. That is the "low level." When I say the Course is written on a low level, what I mean is that it is pitched to all of us who believe we are here. As I frequently say, the very fact you think you are a person reading this book is telling you, you are on the bottom rung of the ladder or maybe the second rung; outside chance, maybe just barely a toe on the third rung. But you think you are a *person* reading a book that is outside of you, along with the whole myth of how the Course came.

When I call it a "myth," I am not saying it did not happen the way the story has gone. I tell the story all the time. But it is a myth because it is a set of symbols. It is not real. Dreams are not real. It is a nice story. And again, I am not saying the facts of the story of the Course are not the way they have been presented to you over the years, but it is all made up. That is not how it was written, because it is not about bodies. It happened outside of time and space. The story you hear about Helen and Bill, and "There must be another way," and all of Helen's experiences are all very nice within the dream of time and space. There is no time and space! There is no world (W-pI.162.6:2). So it did not happen that way. It is a myth. All of this is about being on the lower rungs of the ladder as *bodies*.

The goal of the Course is step by step to be led up the ladder until we finally get to the top. The Course is written in such a way that every once in a while you get these very beautiful passages that give us a glimpse of what it is like on the top.

Those of you who were here for the workshop on "The Transformed World," I talked about two of those lovely sections, "Where Sin Has Left" (T-26.IV), and "The Forgiven World" (T-17.II) that describe the loveliness of this real world. It uses earthly symbols: birds singing, etcetera, or we join together in "the mighty chorus to the Love of God!" (T-26.IV.6:3) But these are all symbols to denote what is beyond all the symbols: this experience of total peace, which is just a hair's breadth away from Heaven. One of my favorite workbook lessons is the one that says in Part II:

(W-pII.302.2:1-3) "Our Love awaits us as we go to Him, and walks beside us showing us the way. He fails in nothing. He the End we seek, and He the Means by which we go to Him"

The thought is lovely and the words are lovely. The Love that this is talking about is *God.* God is at the top of the ladder; *beyond* the ladder. That is the Love we seek, but His Love is also the *means* by which we come to Him through various symbols. The Course uses two symbols: Jesus and the Holy Spirit. You could use any other symbol you want. *A Course in Miracles* would be a symbol. So God is the Love we seek. At the same time His Love extends in the dream in various forms that become the means by which we come to Him. It is a process.

In a sense, what the Course says is: "This is your house. And this is the house," Jesus says, "which I am leading you to, so you will live here one day." And we say, "Well, I am not really ready to live there yet. Yes, it is a nice house but I am not ready for that yet." And over time, we move a bed in; we move a toothbrush, a bar of soap, a shower curtain. Very slowly, we begin to furnish the house. Maybe we will spend an overnight there, and get out as quickly as we can the next morning. But bit by bit, we begin to furnish the house. That is what the Course helps us to do. Jesus does not drag us there. He is standing at the door.

The Inheritance of God's Son

He says in that lovely passage on page 201 in the text in Chapter 11, section IV:

(T-11.IV.6) Christ is at God's altar, waiting to welcome His Son. But come wholly without condemnation [in other words, you cannot enter God's Presence if you are judging], **for otherwise you will believe that the door is barred and you cannot enter. The door is not barred, and it is impossible that you cannot enter the place where God would have you be.** [This is His house. It is not our home yet, but this is the house.] **But love yourself with the Love of Christ, for so does your Father love you. You can refuse to enter, but you cannot bar the door that Christ holds open. Come unto me** [now this is Jesus speaking to us: "Come unto me"] **who hold it open for you, for while I live it cannot be shut, and I live forever. God is my life and yours, and nothing is denied by God to His Son.**

That is the image that you want to have with you. There is this *beautiful* home, this beautiful mansion. Jesus is at the door welcoming us. At the same time he is with us wherever we are, and he keeps saying, "Bring in something." So there we have our toothbrush and our bar of soap. "Bring in something. Spend a part of each day forgiving someone. You don't have to do a whole thing. Just do a little. Spend one hour without judging. Spend five *minutes* without judging; five *seconds* without judging." But that is bringing in a toothbrush. Try and spend more and more time in this beautiful mansion that Jesus stands at the door welcoming us to, and then realize how much you *do not* want to move in.

That is why you hold onto judgments. That is why you do not let go of grievances. That is why you still indulge one more special love relationship. That is why you forget to do the workbook lesson. That is why you try to solve problems on your own. Just realize, "Yes, I am afraid, and this is a process, and I know that Jesus is standing at the door, opening it, keeping it open and welcoming me there." I cannot lose. It is my home. How long it takes me to move in totally is my decision. He is not dragging me. He is not making me feel guilty.

He is simply saying, "You will be so much happier here. Bring in a pair of socks tomorrow. That is all I ask. Let go of *one* judgment. Open your eyes in the morning and do not think of what happened yesterday." That is all he asks. "Look at how meaningless your thunderous world is, the world of specialness; how little it gives you. Why accept just a few measly crumbs when I am offering you a whole banquet? Why accept the little hovel in which you get wet when it rains when I am offering you this beautiful mansion with central heating and air conditioning? You will be so comfortable here. This is your home. This is where you belong."

"I even hung your picture in it," Jesus says. "It is right next to mine. Just come and look at it. You don't have to stay. Just come and look at it." That is what he is saying. You want to wake up every morning and you want to think of that home and say, "Well, what could I bring there today?" And that takes the form of, "What can I let go of? What ego thought can I let go of today? What grievance am I harboring that is no longer so important, that I realize is really meaningless because it will not bring me to that home? Why do I keep trying to patch the roof in this house, this hovel I am living in, this little hut and it does not work, when I could be living in this beautiful, beautiful mansion?"

It is respecting your fear; it is understanding this is a process that enables you to go at your own pace without judgment and without guilt. It will help you to not judge other people for their ego attacks. That is what that section in the manual is about, "How Do God's Teachers Deal With Magic Thoughts?" And the answer is: you do not judge them; you don't get angry at them (M-17.9). You become respectful of *your* fear, and that will help you be respectful of everyone else's fear, whether they are "good guys" or "bad guys" in the perception of the world. You would recognize that *everybody's* afraid.

If we really want to move into this home, which is the only place we will find real peace, we have to bring everybody with us. See, that is the problem. Jesus says, "I am standing at the door and the door is wide open welcoming you, but you must bring everyone with you." He says right at the end of the text, "Yet this a vision is which you must share with everyone you see, for otherwise you will behold it not" (T-31.VIII.8:5). "This a vision is," the vision of total forgiveness, of sameness. "This a vision is" (ultimately of the real world) you must share with *everyone* you meet, everyone you think of, people who are dead or people who are alive, *everyone*, otherwise you will behold the vision not.

If you really want to come to this beautiful home, as I just read to you, you must come wholly without condemnation. Then be aware that when I hold condemnatory thoughts, unkind thoughts, judgmental thoughts, it is serving a purpose. I *do not* want to go into that home. Because if I go into that home and Jesus shows me my picture and his, there will not be any difference. Then when I bring other people with me and we look at the pictures, there will not be any difference. And then we blink our eyes, open them, and there is one picture. That is what the Course calls *the face of Christ*. That is the universal innocence of God's Son; God's *one* Son.

Recognize that is why we do not want to go in. We want to go into this mansion and see our face! And we want to walk into that home alone or with certain special people. We don't want to bring everyone with us. You cannot enter your home if there are any condemnatory, judgmental, unforgiving thoughts in you. It is really essential that you understand that these thoughts are *purposive*. Other people do not make you angry. Other people, other circumstances, do not repulse you. What is not out there cannot make you angry! It cannot repulse you. It cannot attract you.

We give the world and the people and things and events in it that power so that we could deny our mind's power. The mind's power to decide, "I have had enough of this hovel that I am living in. I now want to come to my real home." That is the fear. Once I see this home and I spend any time there in a state of this love and this peace, I will never accept any of the shabby gifts that specialness offer me. And so to ensure that we never make that comparison and make the obvious and inevitable right-minded choice, we don't make *any* choice.

We think we walk this world as mindless creatures. That is what it means to be a body here. Here is the word "mindlessness" on the bottom of the chart. We walk this world as mindless creatures with no power, and all the power is given outside of us, to make us happy, to make us sad, to bring us pain, to bring us joy, to imprison us, to give us freedom, to give us pleasure. Everything is seen outside. Whenever we feel that something or someone gives us pleasure, number one, we are making ourselves bodies so that we would forget that line right at the beginning of the text in Chapter 1: the only "real pleasure comes from doing God's Will" (T-1.VII.1:4). And "God's Will" within the dream is that our decision-making self choose Jesus or the Holy Spirit as our Teacher. That is the only real pleasure.

I am certainly not saying you should deny bodily pleasures, but bodily pleasures obviously make the body real by definition. There is a *purpose* behind that. We do not do things out of instincts. We do not do things because we are driven by hormones. We do not do things because we are driven by past events. We do things because our mind chooses to make the dream real, to give the body and the world power, and then we conveniently forget that we have done so. Then it *does* appear as if we are at the mercy of forces beyond our control, whether they are forces inherent in other people, other things or in our own bodies. No one and nothing has the power to take the peace of God away from you. That is the bottom line of forgiveness. That is the essence of forgiveness.

That is why I forgive you for what you have not done. You have *not* taken the Love of God away from me. You have *not* taken His peace away from me. If I do not feel that Love and that peace, I chose against it, and we understand now why we choose against it. There is no room for "I." There is no room for my specialness, my unique self, in love, or in the peace of God. Because the peace of God embraces everyone as the same and there is no individuality; there is no uniqueness, there is no differentiation. All perceived differences are seen as illusory: "Nothing so blinding as perception of form" (T-22. III.6:7).

Whenever you become upset, whenever you become anxious about something, remember you are "never upset for the reason you think" (W-pI.5). That is why I always emphasize (and you could tell Jesus I said so), you only have to do two workbook lessons. That is all you have to do, but do them perfectly: "I am never upset for the reason I think" (W-pI.5), and "I could see peace instead of this" (W-pI.34). If you do those two lessons, that is it! The first lesson brings everything back to your mind. That is why I am never upset for the reason I think. I am upset because I chose my *ego*, not because of what is going on in my body or the world around me. And because I am back in my mind, I could choose peace instead of this. That is all you have to know. That is the miracle.

Those two lessons embody the heart of the miracle, which is the name of the book. The miracle says the problem is not what is in your body, or in the world. The problem is what your mind has chosen. And because your mind has chosen it, your mind can choose again. How often in the Course does Jesus say "Choose again"? Over and over again. The very end of the text, as most of you know, is "Choose Once Again" (T-31.VIII). That is the final section. Those two lessons encompass everything. That is what you should think about all the time. If you are *doing* the workbook and you are doing all the other lessons, they all have the same content and the same message.

"A Nod to God"

But that is what you should think of: Jesus is standing at the door that is wide open. His arms are wide open, saying, "Come." And then you need to forgive yourself when you say, "Well, one day I will come. Maybe I will not even bring you a whole toothbrush; just a couple of bristles. I will forgive a little bit. Maybe I will just give you a used tube of toothpaste and not a fresh one, because I do not think I want to live here quite yet." But each day (and this would be very helpful), try to bring something into that house until it becomes your home. Each day, try to bring something. Do at least something.

There is that lovely phrase, "a nod to God" (T-24.VI.12:4). Each day try to give God just a little nod, just a little piece of forgiveness. Just try to do that. If you wake up each morning and say, "I am going to try to at least nod to God *once*," and then after you can get through 24 hours and you say, "You know, that wasn't so terrible," then maybe you would nod *twice*. But, I am serious; try to do *something* that will further your Atonement path. Bring something into that house that you could leave, no matter how small it is.

Nobody is rushing you. Nobody is forcing you. Since there is no time, why would Jesus push you? Why would he demand you be healed today? Therefore, why should you demand other people be healed today? Why should you demand *you* be healed today? *You can be*, but your fear, typically, is too great. So you do it slowly; you do it gradually, you do it gently, you do it kindly and you do it patiently.

I always like to cite those two (there are ten) characteristics of God's advanced teachers; number four and number eight: "Gentleness" and "Patience" (M-4.IV, VIII). As is indicated in the discussion of the ten, you do one, you do all of them. But gentleness and patience are so important. You try to be gentle with yourself, gentle with others, and patient. In the section on *patience*, Jesus describes *patience*: you could be patient when you are sure of the outcome.

You know one day you will be moving into that house. There is that recurring phrase in a workbook lesson that says, "Perhaps today, perhaps tomorrow" (W-pI.124.10:1). But you know one day you will be living in that house and it will be your home. And you also recognize, "I am terrified of that." I am patient with myself; and therefore, I am gentle as I go through every day. And when the day ends, and I am lying in bed ready to go to sleep, and I think back over my day and I say, "You know, I did not do very well *but* I nodded to God once. I thought kindly of this person." And that is enough. Just do one thing.

Leave the faucet running just enough to get *one drip*, just one drop of water every day. That is all you have to do so the pipes will not freeze. Living in the northeast you learn that trick. If you are away for a long time; just a few drops each day. Let's just have one drop every day. Have *one* thought of kindness, and then maybe the next day, you will have two, or maybe you will just do one. You don't feel anybody is standing over you with a whip. Do not let other *Course in Miracles'* teachers or students do that. There is no urgency. Jesus is not doing that. Helen never experienced Jesus as doing that to her. How could certainty require an urgency? "Urgency" means you are not there. Realize you are *already* living in that house.

Christians sometimes say that the Christian message is, "Salvation is here, but not yet." Jesus is already here, he already came, the world is saved, but it is "not yet" because we have not accepted it. We are already living in that home as one Son, but we are still dreaming! We are at home, dreaming of exile (T-10.I.2:1). Part of you wants to end the exile but you are terrified. So you go slowly, and you go slowly. Slow but steady wins the race. The tortoise beat the hare, right?

It does not matter how long it takes you because there is no time. Now, obviously, in your right mind you do not want to stall because it makes you miserable. But you first have to accept the fact that you are insane enough to prefer the misery of the ego and this little hovel you call your home, to the glorious home where Jesus is standing with the door open, waiting for you to come in. That would help you realize: "Why wait for Heaven?" (W-pI.131.6:1; W-pI.188.1:1) How much do I want salvation? But not to ask that question and judge your answer. You want to be gentle, you want to be patient, and you want to be kind.

Kindness is not one of those ten, but it certainly is implicit in all of them. Try each day just to have one nod to God, one kind thought, one kind act, and see it as a way of bringing just one object into this house. That would make your whole life meaningful, and that is how you end the "thunder of the meaningless" (W-pI.106.2:1). You realize, "I can make this meaningless world suddenly become transformed into something meaningful simply by nodding to God once a day, twice a day, fifteen times a day." But to really make every effort to at least have one nod, *one* kind thought, that would go a long, long way. Time's up. See you in the Home.

Made in the USA
Columbia, SC
08 October 2022

69105076R00089